LIGHT
BEINGS

Published by Cosmina Movilescu

Light Beings. Copyright © 2025 by Cosmina Movilescu

All rights reserved.

No part of this publication may be reproduced, distributed, or transmitted in any form or by any means, including photocopying, recording, or other electronic or mechanical methods, without the prior written permission of the author, except for brief quotations used in critical reviews, articles, or other non-commercial uses permitted by copyright law.

Some external quotes and excerpts included herein are drawn from public domain sources, while others are used with permission from their respective copyright holders. All quoted material remains protected under applicable copyright laws unless otherwise noted.

This book is intended to guide readers toward inner peace and support the realization of their deepest desires. The insights and techniques presented are designed to inspire, empower, and encourage personal growth. Results may vary based on individual awareness, intention, and consistency of practice. The author assumes no responsibility for the misuse, misinterpretation, or unintended consequences of applying the material contained herein.

For permissions, inquiries, or additional resources, please contact: cosminamovilescu@gmail.com

First edition

ISBN:
978-1-80541-739-2 - eBook
978-1-80541-740-8 - paperback
978-1-80541-807-8 - hardcover

LIGHT BEINGS

Heaven's Guide to Self-Realization, of the Spirit, in the Physical World

COSMINA MOVILESCU

I've always been an extraordinarily good listener,
but not as good at expressing my thoughts.
So, today I would like to dedicate this book,
to all those who are willing to "listen".

Seek what sets your heart on fire, then do your part, and God will do His.

Acknowledgments

First of all, I would like to express my deep gratitude to my fiancé for supporting me from day one, for not letting me give up until I fulfilled my dream. I must admit that he played a significant role in this book's completion and without his unwavering belief and encouragement, I would not have been able to achieve this. You fill my life with light, love, and joy every single day. Thank you for choosing me as your life partner.

My heartfelt thanks to my wonderful sisters, as they have been my pillars of support at all times. I want you to know how honored I am to be able to call you my sisters and also, I consider you my best friends, the kind that anyone could wish for. Thanks to my dear brother, who is at the beginning of his journey and for whom I wish these lines to serve as a guide in the future.

I extend my sincere appreciation to my parents for raising and taking care of us as best they could, for giving us the freedom to choose and make our own decisions about the future, because I strongly believe that this is the most beautiful gift a parent can give to their child, letting them choose the path on their own.

Special thanks to my grandmother, who taught me to be strong in the face of all the adversities that arise every day, to have constant faith and to always hope for the best. And whom I would like to congratulate in this way, for the beautiful age of eighty, turned a few months ago.

I want to express my gratitude to all the wonderful people, full of kindness and love, who I have met throughout my life. To those who are still next to me, but also to those who have left in the meantime. Thank you for being there for me, for the love and time you have dedicated.

In appreciation of the guidance and wisdom provided by all the teachers and great mentors of all times and who have inspired and motivated us to aim higher. Who have dedicated their lives to research, to making this world a better place and for deciding to share the teachings and greatness with all of us. In memory of Bob Proctor, whose inspiration fueled this work and because of him, today I am a better person. Even if I had no opportunity to meet him in person, I felt him very close to my heart.

I am sincerely grateful to the entire team at Publishing Push for their dedication, professionalism, and unwavering commitment. From the meticulous editing to the thoughtful design and seamless production, their efforts have brought this book to life in the best possible way. This journey would not have been the same without each of you, and I am honored to have had such an amazing team supporting this project. Thank you for making this dream a reality.

And last but not least, *you*, dear reader, who took the time to read this book and for giving me the opportunity to tell you my story. I trust that starting from today, your days will be filled with light, harmony, and peace, and above all, you will be very, very, very happy.

Thank you all, from the bottom of my heart.

Contents

Introduction		1
Chapter 1	The AWAKENING	7
Chapter 2	Walking Through the Darkness	21
Chapter 3	The DECISION	39
Chapter 4	The CHANGE	55
Chapter 5	Stepping Toward the Light	71
Chapter 6	Hell Vs. Heaven	87
Chapter 7	The CREATOR	107
References		131
Recommended Reading		133
About the Author		135

Introduction

Have you reached that point in your life when you feel lost, stuck, and nothing works well for you, no matter how hard you try? Do you ever get the overwhelming feeling that your life is starting to fall apart? What if I tell you that I found out the reason why this is happening and not only that, but the solution itself? You already know all this, but you just need to remember, as I did.

All my life, I've been searching for answers, and now that I've discovered the *why*, I feel an undeniable calling to share it with the world. Once you understand, a new path will open. One where miracles unfold all around you, and where you'll be empowered to help those around you too. Stay with me to the very end, as each chapter reveals an important step on your path of transformation, and together we will ignite a profound, lasting change.

Through my own research, I have created a guide that shares personal examples and thought-provoking questions, offering you the tools to embark on a journey of self-improvement and achieve the results you desire. At the same time, I encourage you to embrace change, pursue your goals with confidence, and explore the transformative possibilities of self-realization.

In this writing, I have poured my heart and soul, and I sincerely hope it proves to be helpful to you, as it is filled with love and genuine intention. I firmly believe that anything is possible in this world if you truly want it, especially once you discover the path to inner peace.

The content of this book is the result of my personal research, which I now wish to share with all those seeking the meaning of life. It addresses the questions of why some have everything while others have nothing, and how you can be among those who experience life's wonders without requiring colossal effort. It also includes valuable insights that brilliant minds have shared over time, as well as strategies that successful people have implemented in their lives because they know these principles work.

What were you before you were human? How can you, as a spirit, make this human experience more enjoyable? I dreamed of a figure of light who told me that abundance flows endlessly before me and so if I want to enjoy it, all I have to do is take a step forward. To be part of greatness.

What do you really want? What's stopping you from doing it? Are you ready to step into the light and completely transform your life? Are you willing to become the best version of yourself and be a part of greatness? Everything starts working in your favor once you realize you are destined for wonderful things. Can't you see that if you slow down for a moment and look up? You are a radiant light being.

This book will guide you on a transformative journey of self-realization and personal development, combining practical steps with spiritual insights. Rooted in the teachings of great minds such as Bob Proctor, Earl Nightingale, and Neville Goddard, this book blends philosophy, psychology, and spirituality to highlight the importance of self-knowledge and the realization of one's potential. Through this understanding, we gain clarity in defining our purpose and direction in life.

The seven chapters that encapsulate this book will primarily focus on the importance of being prepared for change, under-

Introduction

standing who you are, and knowing where you are heading. They will also address the necessity of building self-confidence, letting go of the past, and focusing on the present. To attract and create your ideal future, you must first become aware of your own power. This book can provide answers to a large number of questions, including:

- How to deal with anxiety and what your body is trying to tell you.
- Why people face blockages and how to overcome them.
- How to make fear and doubt gradually disappear and live in harmony at all times.
- How you can come to live in a state of alignment and deep inner peace.
- How to heal and genuinely discover true love.
- And last but not least, how to align with the natural flow of abundance.

I assure you that by the end of this journey, you will have gained a deep understanding of your true and authentic self, as this guide is specifically designed for transformation and expansion. This is not just another self-help book, but a guide brought from Heaven, with the intention of helping you live a harmonious life.

I must warn you that what the content of this book reveals could turn your entire existence upside down. Everything you've experienced so far, all the beliefs you hold, may not even be remotely real. If you believe you are ready, then there is nothing left but to embark on the journey of understanding. In order to do this, the only requirement I have is that, before we begin, you question all the beliefs you hold about this world. There are so many things I wish to share in this confession, and I hope to encompass them all, as each one is essential to the process of transformation.

CHAPTER 1

The beginning of all wonderful things is awakening. The moment you become aware, you have accessed the power to become absolutely everything you can be.

The AWAKENING

"If you are ready for the secret, you already possess one half of it; therefore, you will readily recognize the other half the moment it reaches your mind."

– Napoleon Hill, *Think and Grow Rich*

Every time I find myself observing others, I wonder what they think in those moments when they are fully present and not distracted at all. Do they question their existence as I do? Do they feel special in some way? Do they believe that somewhere out there is something waiting to be discovered, the greatest secret of their nature?

Somehow, my intellect has never accepted the term "limited", even though things often seem impossible to achieve. I firmly believe that if you ask yourself the right questions, the answer will come to you in one way or another, and you will find a way.

Everything starts working in your favor once you realize you are destined for great things. The moment you have the absolute conviction that the thing you long for will come true and you no longer have the slightest doubt about it, you will stop rushing and you will start living and enjoying every moment of your life. Peace will naturally arise as you awaken your inner power.

I've always lived with the feeling that there has to be something more than that. I hoped that sooner or later the day when I would discover something great would come and I would end up changing my life. But how far am I from the truth and what is it? This question has haunted me since I was a child. No matter how hard I tried, I felt like I couldn't find my place anywhere and I didn't understand how others could do it so easily and why I couldn't. I was trying to understand what makes us so different from one another. In my mind the same questions ran over and over again: *Am I this?* Followed by: *Is that all?* I never wanted to accept this. It had to be more than that. It all seemed so flat, so gloomy and so erased. Like a movie made in a hurry, with actors you don't believe and action that doesn't move you. Like an illusory reality I could say, which we are experiencing by the way.

The beginning of all wonderful things is awakening. The moment you become aware, you have accessed the power to become absolutely everything you can be. The one who does not step into the unknown will remain asleep and will continue to live as an ignorant person. Our problem is we are waiting for things to happen to us. We do nothing to change our condition. We are so thirsty for the truth and yet, there are so many who let themselves be carried away by fate, and some of us live like this for the rest of our lives. Why do we do this?

I've seen people sitting out on the terrace of the bar at seven o'clock in the morning and most of them aren't even there to have a drink, but just to be away from home. They simply sit there and wait for someone to pass by with whom they can interact. They ask all kinds of questions and are interested in the general condition of those people, what they did yesterday, or what they will do later on, but they know nothing about themselves and they do nothing with their lives. Each of us has enormous potential and all we do is waste it out of ignorance. Most of us know how to live a better life, but we do nothing about it.

The AWAKENING

Do you often feel drained of vitality? Does it seem like nothing you do turns out the way you expect, leaving you with a sense that everything is in vain? Do you struggle to see the bright side of things, often finding yourself clouded by negativity and gloomy thoughts? Do you feel unworthy of anything good, constantly doubting everything and everyone, and no matter how hard you try, you find it nearly impossible to gain clarity and make the right decisions? All of this is a clear sign that you are not fully aligned with your soul's purpose.

We are all endowed with phenomenal powers, yet so few truly understand what that means. Those who do live in a state of grace, empowered, present, and blessed. Those who don't often endure life in quiet torment, always searching but never finding. Many exist somewhere in between, living unconsciously, achieving success without fully understanding why, and unable to explain or teach others how to follow the same path. Well, I don't believe there is just one secret. I believe the difference lies in living with intention and expecting to succeed. As you continue reading, you will uncover the key principles that shaped my own path, and I hope they will help illuminate yours as well.

Many who read these words may not fully grasp their meaning, not because they are too young or too old, but simply because they are not ready yet. If you place a seven-year-old child next to a seventy-year-old adult and ask them the same question, you might be surprised by their answers. Understanding does not come with age, but from knowing one's own nature and true essence. Age, in itself, is irrelevant. As someone once said, wisdom does not necessarily come with the aging process. With age, you simply get older, and that is all.

Wisdom is the ability to act appropriately in a specific moment, combined with the patience to observe everything in its natural state. You cannot live fully unless you begin to orient yourself toward that which lies beyond yourself. When you were a child, your mind was not conditioned by anything, and your heart was open to all possibilities. Children live in absolute fullness, but then they take everything from experiences, from what they see and from what they are told. The power that the intellect gives us is priceless, but we condition ourselves as we grow. We do nothing but limit our potential through the negative beliefs we adopt and accept as true. We deny our own well-being. We reach adulthood and it seems that our only goal is to try to survive as long as possible. Gradually, we end up losing ourselves and the only way to find ourselves is through awareness.

Surely, it has been brought to your attention that to some extent you behave differently with each person you interact with. There cannot be two people who perceive you the same because each relationship is unique, whether we are talking about romantic, friendly, or family ones. You are different and you are totally someone else to any of them, but that does not mean you are a multitude of characters or that only one of those identities is real, but that is how you are perceived by each of them. No human being will be able to fully know another, because each one has a unique vision of all the things and beings that surround them.

You have the ability to significantly change absolutely everything around you if you allow yourself to look at it from a completely different perspective and analyze everything exactly as it is, as if you were born today and know nothing about anything. In other words, imagine waking up this morning and not remembering anything at all, as if you were suffering from amnesia. How do you think you will be and how do you think you will act as a person who has no beliefs or convictions, who has no regrets or fears? You will begin to live as a completely different person than you were before and it will be much easier for you to orient yourself toward the things you feel a special connection to.

Through awareness, you have the power to challenge every thought. By giving yourself permission to alter your thoughts and the way you perceive the world, you have entered a space where the impossible has become possible and so you now have the power to drastically change your life. Awareness is the only thing that can change absolutely everything for us. It is a powerful force for change that has the power to transform everything by shaping our perspective and deepening our understanding. Cultivating it is a lifelong journey of growth that allows us to see the bigger picture, live more consciously, and make better decisions.

Most of the time when I ask someone what the main reason is for why some people have everything while others don't, they answer that it's because they are lucky or they were in the right place at the right time. I would rather say that it is not a mere coincidence but they specifically seek to be so.

When I was about eight or nine years old, I went to the bookstore together with my mother and my older sister to buy some school supplies. My sister chose to purchase a certain model of pen, but I had chosen a different one instead. By the time I got home, mine turned out to be broken. I still remember the disappointment I felt at that moment, because I loved calligraphy and couldn't wait to use that pen. I could hear my mother talking to my stepfather in the next room: "This child is so unlucky; nothing goes right for her. Life is so unfair to her." They were talking about me. I don't know if my mother really believed what she had said at the time, but I started to believe it right from that moment and that's probably the reason why I never got involved in anything, because I thought it wouldn't happen, not in my case.

Children don't know how to tell the difference between what's real and what's not and adults often use all kinds of momentary expressions that children don't know how to distinguish from true beliefs and interpret everything wrong.

We all have different convictions and ways in which we perceive life. A conviction can by definition refer to the certainty or belief that a person has about something. An idea imprinted in our subconscious with certainty, assurance, and firmness and about which we would say that we have enough evidence to consider it true. And yet, what do I mean when I say you need to be prepared? Well, I mean waking up.

And what do we need to wake up? To be willing to change and be prepared to adapt and grow. To turn our attention inward and cultivate the ability to remain in a state of self-awareness. To discover the unknown and to cross the threshold of the beliefs we have adopted throughout our existence. As you increase your level of awareness and become more conscious, you will be able to notice all those things that have kept you stuck all this time. Awakening is nothing but realizing. It is to be able to see something in total, enlightening clarity and to have conscious mental experiences.

We come into the world in a state of unconsciousness and numbness, asleep, but with all the wisdom and knowledge stored in our subconscious without even being aware of it. The truth is we don't see ourselves as we really are, what we are, or who we are. When we wake up, we become more aware of everything that surrounds us, as well as our thoughts and emotions. Awakening occurs precisely at the moment when you discover who you are beyond names, professions, abilities, associations, or characteristics. Stay with me until the end and I'll explain more about this in the last chapter.

The AWAKENING

I have encountered countless moments in which I have thought about something specific and then heard or read that same thing somewhere else. It's downright impressive or even terrifying, some might say. I would dare to say that we all form one mind. We are all talking about the same thing, but it all comes down to what we understand from it. It is necessary to ask ourselves questions of all kinds so that we can then observe and perceive our own existence. Moreover, by asking ourselves the right questions, not those that bring with them even more confusion, but those that bring clarity to our lives and guide us toward the realization of our deepest desires.

I think we've all had an idea or a thought and believed we were the first to think of it, but then realize there were actually others who did before us. When I started to realize this, I began to read more and use this indispensable global network, the so-called internet, to search for the ideas I had. It was the only method I could think of at that moment through which I could discover what I was trying to tell myself. To be honest, it wasn't easy at all. It may sound silly, but in order to find something, you first need to know what you are looking for.

And just to make a quick parenthesis, I'd like to mention that learning new languages has greatly expanded my access to knowledge. Before, I was limited to my mother tongue and Spanish, but now I can explore so much more. I encourage you to study more languages and open new doors to information and opportunities.

I heard Rhonda Byrne saying: "You can't experience anything in life that's outside of your own beliefs." These words had a huge impact on the way I perceived life. Everything finally made sense, my mind lightened, and I began to see everything clearly. I was able to see everything I couldn't see before.

I could not tell you exactly what the moment was when my mind clicked. In my searches, many moments of revelation presented themselves and all of these, one by one, came together to form an accumulation that produced an impressive change in me. There are people who do not believe in change, always exclaiming that one never changes, and I probably would have said the same thing if I did not have myself as an example. I'm not who I was ten years ago, five years ago, or last year, not even yesterday. I have changed tremendously over time. I continue to do so and if I look back, I don't know who that person I was before is. All I do now is nurture this feeling of well-being and share it with others, helping them feel the same way and watching them bloom.

Your reality may not be as bad as you see it through the lens of your eyes, but it's because that's how you think it is. You are surrounded by extraordinary things, and miracles await at every turn, but your dark mindset prevents you from seeing them. Opening your heart is the first thing you need to do, because if you don't, you won't be able to notice anything at all. The second step is to change your thinking and shift your perspective.

Change can happen in infinite ways. We are all unique and it is different for each person, but you have to allow yourself that. Open yourself up to possibilities. If you continue to think and act like everyone else, you will probably stagnate and never get to fulfill your dreams. In order to change your life, you first need to change your perception and the way you see the world. That means being prepared, questioning all your beliefs, everything you thought was true, and opening yourself up to change. It's about doubting everything you know and believe, finding the opposite version of that thought, and then comparing them. This way, you will gain clarity in your thoughts and step onto the path to the world you have always longed for.

You don't want to live as a victim your whole life, so take responsibility for your current circumstances and start taking action to change them. You won't get any different results unless you do, and nothing will help if you won't stop playing the role of victim. You need to understand that you are the only one responsible for everything that happens in your life, and I say this with an open heart. If you can't accept and see things as they are, you won't be able to change them. What do you focus on most of the day? What do you invest your time in? When unexpected circumstances arise in your life, how do you handle them?

According to Ralph Waldo Emerson, the "law of laws" is the law of cause and effect. I will try to explain this simply by asking: "Why did what happened happen?" We reap the consequences of our repeated decisions and actions, and we will not see different results unless we become aware of it before we act in any way. Good deeds and intentions bring positive results, so if you want to change the trajectory of your life, you absolutely have to change your behavior patterns. Absolutely no one is a victim in this world, unless they think they are. Through the power of belief, you can either be blessed or cursed. You have the ability to choose. You must understand that everything you experience in this life stems from what you truly believe in the depths of your being. The things that appear in your life are there, either for you or because of you. You are the one who brings them to life through the nature of your beliefs.

It all comes down to your assumptions. I used to feel really uncomfortable discussing this, but that is no longer the case. I've had strange dreams since I was a child, and they frequently involved future events or things that were quite difficult to describe. I call it a vision hack, as it allows me to analyze and change the end result if needed. Five years ago, a man appeared in my dream, and to summarize, somehow he had all the answers. While we were talking, he turned around for an instant, and as I looked more closely at his notes, what I saw astounded me. I questioned him: "How do you know all this?" He responded: "You will comprehend as you follow." A fire alarm rang in the room we were in, and the last thing he said before he left was: "There's no way I'm coming back here, but I'll meet you on page twenty-three." I remember talking with my younger sister about my dream that night, and she was curious to hear what I thought it all meant. I searched for the meaning in every book I could get my hands on until I found it. The book is called *The Power of Awareness* by Neville Goddard. On page twenty-three, chapter five, *The Truth That Sets You Free*, it states: "The drama of life is a psychological one in which all the conditions, circumstances, and events of your life are brought to pass by your assumptions."

You can't convince anyone to see something they don't allow themselves to see. You have to choose to open up on your own initiative, otherwise you won't be able to do it. There are people who think that what I am trying to say is pure madness, but I know that I am not the only one and that before me there have been others who have discovered this and I would like you to be one of those who do not give up so easily. Indeed, it is hard to believe that it can be that simple when all your life you have tried to overcome and give everything from which you then gain nothing. Yes, it's hard to believe that it can be that simple, but in reality, all these things I'm talking about and that are being revealed to you today have been in front of us all along, but we just couldn't see them.

If you try to analyze for a second each religion or each belief, you will realize they do nothing but fight in an attempt to prove which of them is closer to the truth. Religions, mystics, and the great thinkers of the ages speak of one thing. In a different way, using different words and expressions, but if we pay enough attention, we will realize everyone is talking about the exact same thing.

Never try to convince others to go in search of the truth; they will see it when they are ready. When they wake up, when they are open and aware, only then will they be able to understand and recognize the truth. You will be disappointed to see that those whom you thought were ready are actually far from it, and it's not their fault. We've all been there before we got into the knowledge. If you allow the outcome to speak for itself, you may eventually capture their attention and awaken their interest, and perhaps they will choose to apply it in their own lives as well. In my case, the change began by listening to the beloved Bob Proctor speaking, followed by many other mentors of prosperity, whose teachings, put into practice, radically changed my perception of the world.

One of the key mentors I've been studying and whom I feel I resonate with is Rhonda Byrne, whose journey of writing *The Secret* began by reading *The Science of Getting Rich* by Wallace D. Wattles. This was the start point of my search and study interest that followed Bob Proctor, Earl Nightingale, Joseph Murphy, Neville Goddard, Napoleon Hill, Joe Dispenza, and many more. Then I began to develop my own concepts and ideas little by little, which I captured in this book. The science of the mind is, in my opinion, the most fascinating topic ever studied. That's how I ended up waking up. Once you've reached that point, it's impossible to turn back, and you wouldn't even want to do that anyway. You want to know more, to see more, to be more. You have to feel it in order to understand.

Light Beings

You will comprehend as you follow. By this, I mean: study and apply. Each return to the same material reveals more, which is why I keep coming back to it. Each time I do, my awareness expands and my understanding deepens.

CHAPTER 2

Blessings often come in disguise, yet with patience and calmness, you will be able to notice the lights that are shining on your path.

Walking Through the Darkness

"Remember, it is the world within, namely your thoughts, feelings and imagery that makes your world without."
— Joseph Murphy, *The Power of Your Subconscious Mind*

Our destiny is written in an infinity of versions and with infinite possibilities, but it is up to us which of them we choose to experience. People claim they cannot help but feel tense when faced with external events, but they fail to realize that what they perceive outside is what was originally inside. What you see on the outside, all that chaos is caused by what is already housed inside you. Instead of being an external influence as we would have thought, our worlds are actually a reflection of our inner states. The outcome is directly influenced by what you feel inside; this is the reason for all your suffering. Depending on what you feed it, your mind can work for or against you. You will continue to search in all the wrong places somewhere outside of you, until you realize everything you see on the outside has to do with what is already housed inside you.

There are people who spend their entire lives trying to create an intangible image of themselves, an image so far removed from what they really are, an image based on what some would consider great or admirable. When you try so hard to create a perfect self-image, when you do things just to make yourself liked by others, all you really do is move further away from who you really are, until you reach the point where you no longer recognize yourself and no longer know who you are.

More than a decade ago, sometime around 2010, I was in the locker room of the high school sports hall with my classmates and our headmaster, a physical education teacher at the time. Not having a classroom, we used to meet in the sports hall to attend the tutoring class. Usually, we would have debates on different topics or all kinds of educational activities were prepared for us, but this time it was different. That day was to be a memorable one, but I didn't know it until a few years later.

Our teacher entered the locker room and asked us to listen carefully. He gave us a brief introduction to universal laws, specifically the law of attraction, and presented us with a practical implementation for manifesting what we desire, including the million-dollar bill trick attributed to Jack Canfield. I tend to think he was talking about the famous documentary called *The Secret*, although I never asked him that. I was really fascinated by the subject and had a touching admiration for this man, thinking: "This man is so intelligent." I had no idea what he was talking about, but the vibration his words conveyed to me made me believe that what he was saying was as real as possible. At the end of the class, he handed us each a piece of paper and asked us to write how we see ourselves in five years, giving us a few minutes to write down our ideas. I was simply sitting in a corner enchanted by everything that was happening around me. I could see on most of my classmates' faces that they were as determined as ever about the future. It was only then that I realized I hadn't even thought about it. I had no idea what I wanted to do even in the summer that was to come, let alone in five years. I returned the note on which I had written the first idea that crossed my mind, just to hide my shame and insecurity, even though the notes would remain anonymous.

I immediately recognized him as an exceptional mentor from whom I could learn a lot. My lack of confidence made a mocking voice echo in my head, questioning my IQ. I was so afraid of the impression that this man would have created about me that I preferred to show zero interest in this subject and I continued to do so in various other circumstances over time. The truth is I had not gotten to know myself well enough to realize who I was and what I was capable of.

When you notice a good mentor, ask them to guide you. Try to spend as much time as possible around them and try to surround yourself with people from whom you have something to learn. Surround yourself with people who are more intellectually advanced than you and excel in areas that interest you. A good mentor values their time, but they will be more than willing to help you if they see you are dedicated and disciplined. It's not a shame to admit that you don't know. People learn new things every second of life. Knowledge is infinite and it is downright impossible to excel in everything. The fact that you're interested in evolving is more than enough. In fact, it's all you need; everything else will come naturally as you progress.

What I'm trying to convey is that a lack of confidence in one's abilities and skills prevents people from seizing countless opportunities for growth. Self-awareness and self-acceptance are as crucial as sleep for maintaining good mental and emotional health. Self-confidence and self-esteem are built through knowledge, which comes from both study and direct experience. The one who proudly walks around claiming to know everything, in reality knows much less than the one who remains silent.

I finished high school two years later and moved to Spain. Well, I was always on the road, traveling frequently. At that time, I was that kind of naive, distrustful person with the impression that I didn't know much to be able to handle things on my own. So, I would have followed anyone's advice if I had become attached or close enough to that person. At some point, an inner struggle emerged that would occasionally pull me out of my trance, as I was operating on autopilot and so I had this strange feeling that I was nothing more than a puppet and that everything I was doing was what others told me I should do or what others thought would be best for me. I was so caught up in the chaos that I didn't realize I had been trapped in it for years, until I reached a point where I just couldn't continue anymore.

There was a time when I wished I had pushed myself harder to get out of my comfort zone and not wasted so much time, but to do it right, sometimes you need to be prepared. Maybe I would have learned all these things and much more than I already know. I could have avoided so many moments of embarrassment and suffering, but all the experiences I gained brought me to where I am today and made me see what I couldn't see before.

If we had the possibility to choose to modify a simple small detail about our past, it would change our entire trajectory and the course of our entire existence and we would no longer be who we are today. Hug this old version of yourself and say: "You overcame all the hard work. I am so proud of you." Forget all those things that you think you have done wrong in the past and that you feel ashamed of. At that time, you acted according to what you thought was best, based on the mentality and feelings of that moment, so stop punishing yourself. We should accept everything exactly as it happened, leave the past behind, and focus on the present, because although we cannot change past experiences, we can change future ones. How do you want to present yourself to the world from now on? What can you do today to make tomorrow look different? Act accordingly.

One of the challenges we have faced over time in our personal development is low self-esteem and lack of self-confidence. We tend to compare our abilities and achievements with those of others because we don't know who we really are. If we stopped for a moment to look inside ourselves, we would realize so many things. We have the privilege of experiencing life in the best possible way, but we let ourselves be influenced by all sorts of things that don't really matter and unfortunately, so few can see it.

Some time ago, I saw a recording in which a young lady asked a mentor how she could increase her self-esteem and rid herself of the hatred she had accumulated toward herself. He replied that if she had low self-esteem, it was because she wanted to be better than everyone else.

At first, I was a little skeptical, but then I understood. We blindly compare ourselves to others at every turn, as if we were all the time competing for something. All our achievements, knowledge, or any other things. This need we have to be seen and to convince others that we are capable, that we are worthy of appreciation, exists precisely because we want to be as good as others, if not even better than them. Everything is strictly based on the image you have of yourself.

I have been looking for various methods of personal growth and development over the years. These ideas have been implemented in our subconscious since our earliest years of life. We were constantly told to get better grades, be more involved, be braver, and try harder, always being compared to our siblings, friends, or classmates. Then, in adulthood, the cycle continued, with criticism from bosses at work, friends and colleagues, or even our partners at home.

It took me a long time to find out why I felt this way and then be able to understand it. There are people who face this problem throughout their lives without realizing how they could fix it. All this happens because they have not yet learned how to channel their thoughts and emotions. You fill your mind with thoughts that don't even reflect reality, then let yourself be swept away by misguided emotions.

Be aware that your reality is a reflection of how you see yourself. You will only find peace when you stop trying to prove anything to anyone. When you realize that what truly matters is what you think about yourself, every thought and emotion will naturally be filled with peace. You will feel worthy and good enough, just as you are. This is your natural state. There is no need to make any effort to experience tranquility and peace. Effort only arises when you move away from this truth.

Your primary passion should be personal growth. I believe that the best investment anyone can make is in themselves. It's about investing in your mind. If you have ever thought about investing in something, start investing in yourself first of all and then you will never stop. There is always room for improvement. Once you've done that, you're ready to invest in anything else you find valuable.

Let's say you pay a lot of attention to your physical appearance, and that's great if that's what you want and it fulfills you, but don't do it just to be seen and admired. Choose to do this for yourself and not for others. Like books, so are people. A beautifully designed book cover is a crucial element, but if your attitude and personality don't inspire me and I don't see anything beyond your beautiful appearance, then I've lost interest. I'm sure you understand what I'm trying to say. We all completely agree that it's not enough for a book to have just an attractive cover. If we start browsing through it a little and the content doesn't captivate us, then it will return to the shelf. While our outward appearance can convey a lot about us and contribute to a positive first impression, it's our personality that ultimately makes the difference. It would be great if you could maintain a healthy balance between the two and develop them simultaneously. This way you will create a strong and admirable presence.

After living in Spain for a few years, I returned to my native country, and even after more than a year, I still hadn't managed to find my place. I used to be a timid and quiet person, always trying to solve my problems on my own, so I knew very well how to mask any trace of my anxiety. Have you noticed that we always tend to hide from others the fact that we don't feel well and pretend to be strong as if it were something shameful? In the spring of 2017, I reached a point where it was difficult for me to find myself. Have you ever felt engulfed by a mix of melancholy, sadness, regret, and, at the same time, anger, without even having any good reason, but it simply appears out of nowhere? When you experience this state, you feel tired, unable to engage in any type of activity, and you feel that your actions are meaningless. Well, that state had settled in my body almost permanently and I had come to no longer want to be in the presence of other people. I withdrew from the world, limiting my communication to only a few people. I had ended my relationship with my then partner and most of my friendships, and my sole goal was to put my thoughts in order.

No matter what problem you are facing right now, ask for guidance and the solution will be revealed to you. When you free your mind, you gain clarity and inner guidance. When you are in a dark place, the idea is not to search for a light source, but to be the light yourself.

Months later, I had reached a point where I was afraid to sleep because I had been suffering from sleep paralysis almost every night for months. If you have ever experienced this, you know how terrifying it can be. In my case it manifested itself in all possible ways, and I woke up every night crying and screaming. There were nights when I woke up to find my mother sleeping with her head on the edge of my bed and holding my hand, even though she would wake up before sunrise the next morning. I didn't understand what could be causing all this, but I knew it was something that needed my immediate attention.

I had effectively lost control of all these states and sensations shrouded in chaos and terror. This feeling of emptiness and division had taken hold of my entire being, and it was impossible for me to find a way out. And to be honest with you, I never believed in the term depression. But if you analyze the state I was going through at that time, you could say that I described exactly the same thing. The main cause of these unfortunate episodes was none other than stress and anxiety. Before, I lived with the impression that it was just a form of complaining or begging for attention and that in reality there was no such thing. Some people claim that it is impossible to control these states and that they flow like a river from which most often, without professional help, it is impossible to get out.

I would say that it is nothing but fear and confusion. I was downright terrified of this unwanted future that was running in my mind endlessly, and yet I was the one who had created this harmful vicious cycle that was causing all my suffering and mental fog. Although it originates in the mind, emotional suffering can be just as painful as physical suffering. You become the prisoner of your own prison and the only one who can free you from there is you. You have to understand this. Fear is what paralyzes you and transports you to the darkest places. Once you overcome that barrier, you simply free yourself and everything that you apparently considered impossible to deal with will vanish.

These states can also be generated as a result of trauma, suffering, or internal chaos that has intensified over time, of which you are most likely not even aware. If we talk about the manifestation of a trauma, it is very likely that the trauma that causes you so many blockages and that prevents you from moving forward has not even been experienced personally, but has been transmitted over generations.

If you agree with the above, take the time to identify the cause of these symptoms. You'll have a pretty uncomfortable experience going through this whole process, but as soon as you track down the cause, you'll not only be able to find a way to prevent it from triggering, but you'll be able to eliminate it directly from the root. In the sixth chapter, I'm going to talk more about it and I'm going to introduce you to some factors that will seem insignificant at first glance, but that are terribly important and which, if you follow, will make a huge difference and your life will take a turn that you could not have even imagined.

You would probably understand much better if I mention some of the details that underlie everything behind the suffering that I experienced, but I am not going to bore you with elaborate details and the truth is that it will not be of any use to you. All it will do instead is give them even more power. I would advise you not to do it either, not to focus on the problem, and if you have to look into your past, do it only to reflect and find a solution or to free yourself from all that accumulated burden. Spend time with yourself and observe how your body reacts to whatever you do. The best answers you will ever find are nowhere else but inside you. Just listen carefully.

There are people who complain constantly, but do nothing about it. It's just a habit they have formed over time and they don't want to break from it. Often, they seek compassion, choosing to remain in the victim state, but no one wants to be in the company of these people, but rather run away from them. I would urge you not to talk about your problems constantly and repeatedly with anyone, whether they are your friends or family. You will do nothing but arouse in them reasons for concern and even more so, make them also focus on the problems that they also have.

You must take responsibility for your decisions and actions, and if you decide to talk about your things with others, never do it with the intention of complaining, but with the aim of finding a solution or helping others bring more clarity in their lives. I'm not saying that you shouldn't share your emotions and feelings with other people. It's totally okay to ask for help when you need it and maintain an emotional connection with your loved ones. If things go really wrong for you, keep in mind that sometimes no matter how much others want to help you, they won't be able to do it and not because they don't want to, but simply because they don't know how to do it, and in this case, it would be better to seek professional advice.

There are so many triggers and so many ways in which anxiety can manifest itself. For each person it is different and if you think you can't cope on your own and you need help in detecting the cause, find a specialist, someone who can guide you and free you from all this mind burden. However, I want you to understand that you are the only one who can make a change and no one else can do it for you, no matter how hard they try. It is an exclusively internal matter.

I felt that I had no one to talk to about what was happening in my life at that moment. But every time, somehow as if by miracle, wonderful and kind people always appeared in my path who, through their way of being, brought me joy and hope in the most difficult moments. There are people who appear in our path and unconsciously change our lives. Some of us don't even realize the impact that others have on us. You have to know that you can always find support outside of your environment, even though you get the impression that no one can help you. I first discovered it in books, and then I started following those people online who inspired me and helped me change.

It's like I died a few times because of the suffering, the emptiness I felt inside, and because of the lack of love from others toward me. I thought I was suffering because others couldn't see how much I cared and what I was doing to make them happy. Later I realized that the main reason for my suffering was that I didn't know how to love myself. In this way, you can't even feel the love that others have for you; all you are doing is blocking it both ways.

The lack of self-love is the main reason why you feel miserable. Once you start to truly love yourself and see yourself with admiration, then you will learn to love others and feel the love they have for you back. There may be a few things you need to change first to get to that position where you are satisfied with yourself and your results, but consider that as human beings, we will always be seeking to evolve and become better. Keep this in mind when criticizing yourself and try to maintain a balance between criticism and adoration.

It is almost impossible for a person to change completely overnight. If you want to change, you should know that in the first instance you will feel quite uncomfortable and powerless. You will have the impression that nothing goes well; it will seem to you that things are going even worse and you will feel the need to withdraw and return to what you were doing before. Yet, if you are persistent and patient, you will be able to get through it eventually.

While this may not be the best example, it makes me think of when you start a diet. The difference between the two will be that one happens on a physical level, and the other on a mental and emotional level. When you start a diet, the worst thing you can do is suddenly start eating only healthy foods after consuming for a long time lots of foods that were harmful to your body. The best option is to try to eliminate them gradually, otherwise you will start to feel sick and end up creating a real problem if you won't give your body enough time to adapt. The same goes for your emotions. For example, if you are the type of person who loses your temper easily, trying to control yourself and refrain from doing so will only make the situation worse and you can end up creating a much worse scene even if your intention was a positive one. Your body has become accustomed to what it has been fed so far and to change this you have to do it in small, patient, and repetitive steps. This is how you end up reinventing yourself. The way to succeed in all aspects of life is to adopt a certain way of living and being.

Maybe one day a thought like this will come to your mind: "Is there something wrong with me?" You may be wondering this right now, or you may have been believing this for a while and often have the thought: "I'm the problem. I already know this." Then you're most likely already at the stage where you've come to blame yourself for all the things that are happening right now in your life, because you've chosen to let them happen and not intervene when they went in the wrong direction. Stop blaming yourself. That is who you were in the past. Bob Proctor used to say, "You are the only problem you will ever have and you are the only solution." Remove from your mind all those thoughts that are holding you back from moving forward, because they are part of the past, and focus on what you can do right now to change those things. Start from scratch and do it in the best possible way right now, being and acting like the best version of yourself. This is the only way, and therefore you cannot go anywhere else but upward.

All my problems stopped the moment I realized that this emotion called anxiety was not an enemy or something problematic that I had to deal with, but rather a companion. A friend who constantly reminds me that I am absent, that I am not living in the present moment, but rather wandering up and down thinking about my future, trying to predict what will happen next. We often spend too much time thinking about the past and the future. Your perspective on the world can be changed by living in the present and finding beauty in simple things. The worry and emptiness you feel in your chest are there only to guide you and help you get back on track. To remind you that your only purpose here is to enjoy the journey. Focus on what you truly want instead of what you are trying to avoid. Every time your mind wanders and begins to worry, remember to return to the present moment, to what is truly meaningful, and focus on the things you can do right now.

One day I went to a friend's house and had a few drinks. I wasn't used to doing this and it had most likely been the first or second time in my life when I had more than two glasses. I arrived home a little before midnight in a rather unpleasant condition. My mother looked at me, unable to understand what had really happened to me. I could see the disappointment settle on her face, while asking: "What's wrong with you? Are you really not thinking?" And yes, she was right. I wasn't thinking at all. I was doing everything mindlessly. I didn't care at all until I saw the concern and disappointment in her eyes. Sometimes I think that in order to get to live in paradise, we must first go through hell. It seems that we were all there at some point, when we got acquainted with suffering. I went to the bathroom, I looked in the mirror, and I saw all the sadness behind the bad mood and, encouraging myself, I said: "I know who you are and this is not you at all." And that night I promised myself that I would do everything in my power to get to the moment when bliss, peace, and joy would rule over my entire being.

You would say that someone who has suffered numerous physical misfortunes and traumatic experiences would be entitled to sink into suffering. However, I believe that someone who has built a dungeon within their own mind and comes to experience it as a kind of hell may feel equally overwhelmed as the previous one.

Most of the time, the inner struggle and helplessness you feel are not based on any good reason, but manifest themselves only because you don't know who you are and where you are going. All this could not affect us except for this reason. Growth and change live through us and as human beings we continue to evolve, we aspire to more, and we will always have that desire and need to improve our results and overcome our self-imposed limits. If we don't have a specific goal, then how can we be excited about the future?

Other times we end up feeling unjustified because even if we fight hard and put our heart into what we do, things don't turn out as we expected. What you need to know is that once you figure out who you are and have decided what you want to do, nothing can stop you. No one should be in a situation where they don't know what they want to achieve. Only then can you step into the light and come out of the darkness. Sometimes we face all kinds of obstacles, but they only appear to guide us toward what we want to do or become, because we have deviated from the way and taken a path that does not lead to the fulfillment of our dream.

Lack of confidence is most often related to fear. Fear of failure, fear of losing your reputation and being embarrassed, fear of being rejected, all of these do nothing but limit your potential. Change your internal dialogue. Your thoughts, emotions, and actions should never be influenced by the opinions of those around you. Do not accept criticism and be open to learning. The biggest mistake you can make is trying to please others. You do not need anyone's approval to do what you want. Do not take the risk of losing yourself just to receive the validation of others. Continue to progress at your own pace without the need to be seen or validated by others. In reality, it is not their opinion that matters, but the self-image you have and what you believe about yourself. Do not allow anyone to change your state. Don't give anyone the privilege of making you feel the way you don't want to feel, because that's how you give the other person the power to be in charge and manage everything about you as they consider. Why would you do that?

All you have to do is move forward and trust yourself without overthinking or creating countless "what if" scenarios. The progress is not always visible in the moment, but each decision and each action compounds over time. Keep moving forward with confidence, knowing that even the quietest shifts lead to powerful transformations, and remember, the most meaningful changes often happen without us realizing it. So trust the process and trust yourself. As someone once said: "Day by day, nothing seems to change, but when you look back, everything has changed."

CHAPTER 3

Depending on what you feed it, your mind can work for or against you. You will continue to search in all the wrong places, somewhere outside of you, until you realize that everything you see outside has to do with what is already housed inside you.

The DECISION

"You are bound by no fixed form. By the freedom of your own will, you may fall to the level of beasts or rise to the divine, shaping yourself according to your own choosing."
— Inspired by Giovanni Pico della Mirandola,
Oration on the Dignity of Man

Why are people stuck? Why don't they make the decision to change their lives and follow their dreams? Because they don't believe it's possible and that's why they don't do anything. They simply survive instead of trying. Because they are afraid of being disappointed if they don't achieve what they set out to do and that's why. It's quite sad that they don't understand that failure is not necessarily a confirmation that something is impossible to achieve, but rather a step forward, which brings you closer to that fulfilled desire. Experience will teach you numerous lessons, and striving for success will propel you forward and help you discover a path to your destination. Knowing all this, simply get rid of whatever is holding you back and take action. This is the only way to change things around you, by choosing to do it.

What steps should I take to get to where I want to be in life, and what should I change about myself to become the person I want to be? Keep a clear record of each step, where you are now, and where you want to go, so that you can orient yourself toward your desired destination. Our daily decisions determine the kind of life we lead. Those small, insignificant decisions that we make every moment of our lives are what shape our lives.

Every time I have to make a decision, this question that Bob Proctor used to say repeatedly comes to mind: "What do you really want?"

You have to decide what you want to do. Otherwise, it's like being in the airport, running disoriented between destinations without actually going anywhere. How can you get there if you don't first decide where?

If you want to improve the quality of your life, you have to start with yourself. There is only one thing that holds people back and keeps them stuck, and that is their mindset. It all begins in the mind. Your mindset is the seed from which everything else grows. Whether we like it or not, we have to recognize that every event in our lives is the result of a decision we made at some point. There may be things from your past that you weren't entirely responsible for, but if you want to change the course of your life, you must make a decision. You could use all kinds of excuses and remain stuck right there or you could move on. It's your choice.

A detail worth mentioning is that we will always run into blockages. It is inevitable. One reason could be that we are lost in a place where we no longer understand ourselves and because we no longer know where to go and what decisions to make. Another reason arises from the desire to move forward, but not knowing exactly how to proceed. There can be multiple reasons. What we need to understand is that it is normal and we all encounter them, but the idea is to overcome them and not let ourselves be conditioned by them. The roadblock is always between trying and succeeding and if you cross its threshold, you have overcome your conditioning. The greater the desire to move forward and the higher your goal is positioned, the more pronounced the obstacles and impediments will be. Otherwise, it indicates that your goal is not big enough, which means that its fulfillment will not produce a substantial result toward evolution. That is why, many times, even if we have achieved our goal, it does not satisfy us enough. You need to aim higher and pursue what sets your heart on fire in order to achieve great results. Set goals that truly excites and inspires you, and you will achieve results beyond what you ever imagined. However, consider that goals facilitate personal growth and shape your identity; they are not just about the rewards obtained from overcoming challenges.

Identify your dream goals and move with conscious intention, always in pursuit of what your heart truly desires. You need to have a clear vision of what you want and then take deliberate action to make it a reality. You might enjoy financial freedom while also embracing simplicity. Perhaps a small, charming cottage nestled in the mountains, where you reunite with family. A place where you feel deeply connected to all of creation, grounded in balance and peace of mind. Or maybe you are drawn to an exuberant lifestyle in a villa with breathtaking views and a vibrant cultural life. A quiet life shared with an ideal partner, or a dynamic career marked by colossal success. It can be anything, depending on the terms in which you define prosperity and whatever sets your heart alight. We are all different and each of us has a different vision of the perfect life. This means living with intention, feeling truly fulfilled, and letting your experiences unfold as you please. This can change over time, so make sure you regularly review and adjust your vision so you know what you want and where you are going.

Some people say that you have to work hard if you want to succeed in life, but what is that supposed to mean? How do we define a successful person? Some people think that being successful means getting rich and having a lot of money. Well, I think they have nothing to do with one another. The problem is most people don't know what they want, and if they make a decision to do something, it is often based solely on what they could earn in return.

Successful people are those who can live exactly the way they want every day of their lives, without being conditioned by anything. Success isn't about money. It's about living life to your heart's content. Money is simply a bonus. So, when someone tells you that you must work harder and strive more to become successful, they are absolutely right. But only if it means reshaping your mindset, overcoming self-imposed limitations, realizing who you really are, what you really want, and discovering what is holding you back from acting, but not when it refers to obtaining material goods.

I believe the purpose of life is to pursue what you truly love, what excites you enough to make you jump out of bed every day, and truly make life worth living. And which, above all, in addition to bringing you joy, contributes to the well-being of everyone around you. How do we discover what our purpose is? We've all asked ourselves this question at some point and if you randomly ask a few people you will realize most of them are unable to give you an answer and it's because they don't know. If you are one of them, keep calm and do not get discouraged, because this is not something to be found, but rather chosen. Purpose is not about something you achieve, but rather about becoming. Once you decide on your purpose and commit yourself to it, you will realize that you have been truly blessed all along.

As a teenager I used to think that by the time I hit twenty-five I would have a successful career, be happy and fulfilled, meet my soulmate, and become a mum, but when I looked around I had none of that. I was lonely, broke, and depressed.

The DECISION

In an article published on the Proctor Gallagher Institute website entitled "Snap Decisions and Small Things", Bob Proctor mentions that one day, in the mid-sixties, just as he was about to leave the meeting he had with Earl Nightingale, he asked: "Earl, what is the big deal? What is the secret to life?" He smiled and replied: "There is no secret, Bob. It's a simple matter of sitting down and deciding what you want to do with your life and then do it." I love this short story by Bob and I hope it helps you if you are searching for your purpose and have not yet decided what you want to do.

It could be said that we are nothing more than a sum of decisions that we have made over time. So, it was time for me to make a decision. I looked deep within my soul and around me, then I decided that the best option would be to leave for an indefinite period, somewhere where I could experience peace and where I had the opportunity to rediscover myself and start over. I made a meticulous and detailed plan for several months, saved most of my earnings, and decided to move to Spain, but this time to a different part of the country than my previous stay.

Would you also believe that leaving is the best option? In the summer of 2018, I was flying to Valencia. At first everything was enchanting. There was so much to see and explore, but after the first week I had already started to realize that it had never been about the place, the people, or the circumstances, but myself. I was the main reason for all my disappointments. I was the root cause of all my failures, shaped by my past self and the confusion that led to all my disappointments and heartbreaks. There was nothing wrong with that place or those people from my past, but me. It was just the way I saw myself at that time and I felt I could no longer identify myself with the person I left behind. I refused to go back only because of who I thought I was in that place or who I thought I wasn't, as well as because of my actions or lack thereof. I needed this detachment. I wanted to truly find myself. I was able to recognize the need for change once I was alone with myself. I needed to be somewhere where nothing I saw or touched was related to the past. Wherever you decide to go, your emotional baggage will come with all the other things needed for the journey. I think this is true for most of us, and there is absolutely no point in running away to find out who you are. I thought it was much easier this way because I could see everything with absolute clarity, but that doesn't mean it actually was. You won't get anywhere if you keep running away from yourself. The truth is, you must find your own way, because you are the only one who truly knows what's best for you.

You are the one who stands behind all the accumulations. We often hear the phrase: "You need time to pause and simply be." How many of us do that? It's revealing. Imagine a drawer full of all sorts of things, both pleasant and unpleasant, and then try to remove them gently. What remains in the end is you, not only the one without fear, but also without delight. Somewhere in the middle is situated this ideal space that keeps you completely detached from either of the two areas, in a perfect balance immersed in peace and harmony. That is the real you, and all other things are nothing but accumulations.

The time has come to finally be you, the one you truly are. You are confused because you were not yourself from the beginning and because you have not dedicated enough time to yourself to even know. How can you reinvent yourself? The easiest way to do this is to stop identifying with your past self and focus on the new image you have of yourself, until you can see, choose, and keep only those things that serve you, that fulfill you, and that make you happy. And if you do so, there will come a time when you will fully embrace and live it.

When I made up my mind and made the decision, the plan was not just to start over, but to reshape myself entirely. To do this, you need to have the strength to say no to everything that robs you of your peace. The most important thing I did was say no to everything that fell short of my expectations from this new person I was about to become. So, if I had the slightest feeling that something wasn't right, I quit. I started to trust my intuition and followed it. Everything was then based on my intuition and everything I chose to do was according to it. All I do now is based on this, because what is intuition really? It is pure consciousness. That inner voice is your higher self that communicates to you, so follow it. It's you.

What is your most burning desire? If you had all the resources, all the money, and all the opportunities in the world and you had a one hundred percent guarantee of success, then what would you like to do? Most people don't really know what they want, moreover, they haven't even thought about it. If you are in the same situation, it is probably because you have only played a supporting role in your own film and have lived only by chance.

We are so caught up in all this rush and hustle and bustle that we often forget what is really important to us. If you have enough patience and give yourself enough time to think, you will surely be able to discover what you really want to do. Once you discover what you're willing to dedicate your life to, you must realize that it's not enough to simply decide to do it. You must commit yourself fully to the cause, make it your top priority, and work toward it every day until you see it accomplished. The more work you put into something, the more valuable it becomes.

One of the first steps on your journey is to decide what kind of life you want to live. Moreover, the most important step to becoming the person you want to be is to first see yourself mentally as the person you would like to be. I believe that anyone who dedicates time and effort to the goal they want to achieve and commits a hundred percent to it will inevitably be successful, because they will not stop until they achieve it. To be successful, you must do whatever it takes to go to bed better than when you woke up in the morning. It's no use knowing this if you don't put it into practice. What is that thing you have done today that you will benefit from tomorrow? Your future is created by what you do today.

In an article published on Jack Canfield's blog, called "The Power of Being Committed", readers are asked: "Why is it that 100% commitment is the key to success, while even a 99% commitment is a recipe for failure?" Jack Canfield is the man who changed everything for me when he answered this question, because I could see the importance of this small detail and the difference it can make. When you are totally committed to something, you will do it no matter what the circumstances are and you will leave no room for procrastination or giving up on doing it. So, keep this in mind the next time you make a decision. The progress you will make will be lightning fast once you follow and apply this principle to your life.

Most people have no idea what they want, but there are some who do and will tell you with so much enthusiasm what it is, but then add that it's too good to be true, so they never get it. They stop before they even try. I know a lot of people like that. They just don't want to be disappointed if they don't get what they want, and so they refuse to dream. Do you find yourself in the same situation as I mentioned earlier? If so, you need to get that idea out of your head because all you're doing is cancelling all the possibilities. If you try, you might have a chance of success.

The DECISION

How do you know you can't if you don't even want to try? So don't tell me you really want it. If you really, really want it, you'll find a way.

By taking the risk, you give yourself the chance to succeed. By allowing yourself this opportunity, regardless of the outcome, you give that thing permission to enter your life. But by giving up and accepting from the very beginning that you can't do it, it's the same as trying and failing; you will lose either way. All you have to do is make the decision to do it and sooner or later it will come to life. You just have to be patient. Just because it won't be when you want it, doesn't mean it won't happen.

If I ask you if you want to do something and you tell me you don't have time, I'll understand that what I'm suggesting isn't one of your priorities. When you really want to do something, you put it on your to do list as a priority. You'll say: "I'd like to do that but I have to go shopping. I really need something right now." Then tomorrow you'll clean your car and sweep the garage. The day after tomorrow, you'll feel compelled to help someone close to you. Every day you'll have things to do, and so you'll never be able to do what you really want and get involved in what you dream of doing or becoming.

You have to dedicate time to what you want, to do it as if it were crucial and essential, like the need to drink or eat. Set a specific completion date for each goal, respect its completion deadline, and try as much as you can not to postpone. Wake up and do this first thing in the morning, and if you haven't managed to do it, do it before you go to bed. Don't go to sleep before devoting even a little time to the thing you want to see accomplished, and thus, slowly, slowly, you will notice how the image you have in your mind begins to come to life in the physical plane as well.

I always follow my intuition these days and if I feel I should not be there, I simply give up. But be careful not to confuse this feeling with discomfort. It is normal to feel uncomfortable when you are not familiar with the subject, so follow the challenges and trials and you will see that the excitement afterward will be worth all the effort. If you are open to possibilities, you can achieve great things, but only if you act upon it, if you are determined and dedicated. Frustration and impatience are what we feel when we are certain we are one step away from success and yet, nothing happens, but we have to be patient. There is a process in everything.

We often make the mistake of asking others what we should do in different situations: "Tell me, please, how do you think I should proceed in this situation?" We tend to ask questions of this kind when we encounter a problem, but others can only advise us detachedly and only from a point of view of what could be considered beneficial for us, but without any kind of involvement. It is also good to listen to the opinions of others because many times others can help us see things we might not have been able to see. Advice is always welcome and we can take it into consideration, but not to follow blindly. We are the ones who have to make the decisions and the only ones who know what is best for us. Some people spend their whole lives influenced by what others tell them they should do and make decisions based on what they think would be best for them and thus never get to know themselves, to know really what they want, and this is where all the frustrations start.

In the past, I used to listen to the opinions of those around me who told me that I wasn't worthy enough, and that I wasn't capable of doing wonderful and meaningful things in life. When you hear one thing over and over again you inevitably start to believe that thing. This is the power of repetition. It doesn't matter if it's true or not, if you listen and start thinking about it considerably, it will sink into your subconscious and you will have to live with the consequences of this limiting belief. In the next chapter I will talk in more detail about this magical amulet, its impact on us, and how it works.

All the decisions you have made throughout your life have led you to where you are now and have made you who you are today. Don't regret any of them. The regrets you have are in the past; leave them behind. When you worry about what happened yesterday or fear what will happen tomorrow, you neglect today. If you can't accept and see things as they are, you won't be able to change them. You can't change what has happened, but you can change what will come next. Focus on the present and what you can do now.

Life is the sum of everyday decisions. Decisions determine our path in life and can lead to success or failure depending on the belief we have about the outcome. Faith can lead us to achieve our goals, while fear keeps us away from them.

It really doesn't matter where you are right now, it's what you're doing right now. Stop looking back and focus on the now and act in alignment with the person you aspire to become. You may be doing something right now that you've been working on for years, but it's no longer fulfilling you. You're experiencing a blockage right now because you've changed your mind in the meantime, and your desires are different, and there's nothing wrong with that. Allow yourself to change direction once you feel this.

We are stuck in the past and we want a better future, but we don't live in the present moment. We focus our attention on the future, but in order to get the things you want, you have to change and start behaving like the person you want to become by living in the present, otherwise it won't work. We need to replace the old beliefs that no longer define us with new ones that will help us move forward. If you follow the same path as in the past or if you have the same beliefs and paradigms, you will not be able to achieve different results. You have to let go of the past, because the more you think about yourself in the past, the more your past will continue to manifest as future.

Successful people are constantly working to become the best version of themselves and strive daily to surpass themselves. This is the secret of success. I absolutely love what Cristiano Ronaldo shared during his 2022 interview on Piers Morgan Uncensored: "Everyone wants to be Cristiano Ronaldo, but nobody wants to work to be Ronaldo. If I give you the map, nobody will want to do all that work but they want results." Most of us want certain things, but we are not willing to do the work to get there. Discipline is considered the key to success.

The discipline they apply in their lives is what truly drives them to success, not motivation. Their faith keeps them motivated to follow their dreams, and it is obvious that if you don't believe in something, then you won't act on it. Without faith, action is impossible, therefore it is said that everything begins with faith. First of all, you have to believe. Faith is the start of everything you do. It's how you give life to all things, but what makes you move forward and accomplish anything, without a doubt, is discipline.

The moment you decide what your heart desires and you keep your focus on that thing, it will come true, because once you do that, you will automatically do everything that is in your power to see it manifest. Some often say they want a certain thing, but they don't do anything about it. There will always be excuses and inconveniences, but the people who truly succeed are the ones who overcome them and take the necessary steps to advance and thrive. You may think you need to know how to do it first, but in reality you just have to decide to do it, be dedicated, and trust that you will succeed. Most of those who have achieved great things in this world had no idea how to do it. They were probably in a similar situation to yours, but they put all that aside and decided to move forward despite the circumstances. The power of intention is boundless and once you've chosen to make it your top priority, the path will show itself.

There is no point in daydreaming if you do nothing else in this regard. Those who get what they want don't get it just by making the decision to do it, but because they take action to carry out the plan. This is the difference between those who manage to succeed and those who don't. Commitment is the ongoing determination not to give up until you reach your goals and to wake up with the aim of making them a reality.

In *Think and Grow Rich*, Napoleon Hill said: "There is a difference between wishing for a thing and being ready to receive it." Just dreaming and wanting something concrete will not make it appear out of nowhere. You must first find out what you really want, because most people don't even think about it at all. When they do start thinking about it, they cannot stop doing it anymore. As you find out what your burning desire is, you must believe that it can be done and that the goal can be achieved. He also said: "Faith is the only known antidote for failure." If many of your intentions are not carried out successfully, it is because somehow deep down in your heart you doubted it. With a lot of effort and dedication, you may eventually be able to carry out some of the plans you have set, but it should not be like that at all. It has to be made with love, with enthusiasm, and with positive emotions. What you hold in your heart, you draw into your life. The most extraordinary things ever accomplished by human beings have been fueled by the strength of their faith and determination.

CHAPTER 4

You are not seeing this world through your eyes, but your heart. Whatever impression you might have about the world, you should consider this first.

The CHANGE

"You see, you don't attract what you want. Wants are in your conscious mind. You attract what you are in harmony with, what you are. And you are the thoughts that become fixed in your subconscious mind."
— Bob Proctor, Proctor Gallagher Institute,
"The Real Secret to Living the Life You Want"

If you want to change your life, you have to make the decision to do it first and when you understand that the decision is not about what to do, but about who to be, all the other decisions you make after that will be with the intention of getting closer and closer to this ideal image of the person you wish to become. In order to do this, you must induce the idea that you already are the person you wish to become. You must first forget who you are in order to become who you want to be and act according to it.

There have been so many moments in my life when I have spent dozens of minutes with my eyes closed or staring at the ceiling, thinking and analyzing my life. I have always been in search of my true identity and I have tried to find out who I really am. You see, sometimes it's very easy for you to give advice to others, but when it comes to yourself, it's impossible to figure it out. You have to spend time with yourself. It's good to be surrounded by people, but how will you get to know yourself if you don't spend time with yourself?

Not knowing who you are and where you are going is definitely something we don't want to experience. It is normal to feel anxious when we realize that the image we had of ourselves is so far from who we really are. The voice in our head will become clear only when we start looking within our own hearts. Only then will we be able to understand why we act the way we do and we will finally have the power to change it.

Whatever you truly believe in your heart, that is what will surround you through the power of belief. You need to understand the importance of beliefs and the role they play in our lives. Your beliefs and perceptions of reality influence the way you think, feel, act, and, in short, how you live. The results we get and how we live depend on the way of thinking, feeling, and acting, as all of these together make up the way we are. It is strictly related to what you believe and what you consider to be your truth, and ultimately determines the results you get and the way you experience life.

If the life you are living is not fulfilling you and nothing seems to be working, then you should probably change the way you operate. Everything starts with you, and nothing will change unless you change first. Let's say you want to make a stir-fry of vegetables and although the ingredients have been chosen with great care, if the heat is not right, the result will always be disappointing. You could try to repeat the same process over and over again, but you will get the same disastrous result, as you have acted in exactly the same manner as before. If something does not work the way you expected, it is clear that you need to try a different way. It is not about how hard we try or how much effort we put in, but about how we do it. The fruit of your labor will always be the same as long as you do not change your attitude, regardless of your good intentions.

In essence, your thoughts profoundly influence your actions and the direction your life takes. In *The Science of Getting Rich*, Wallace D. Wattles states: "A man's way of doing things is the direct result of the way he thinks about things." Your actions are driven by your thoughts. If your life is a constant struggle and you want to see a change in things and the environment, to live in a totally different way than the way you live right now, you should know that change will always start with you and the change of your inner world. It is necessary for you to change in order to see changes in your life, because things do not change by themselves until you do.

You could argue: "I am who I am, so the ones who truly love me will accept me as I am." You have the ability to grow beautifully in an unimaginable way, so why not do that?

Being and acting like the best version of yourself at all times is the key to living life to the fullest and in the best way possible. It's not about how others see you or the expectations they have of you, but about how you see yourself, about the limits you unconsciously impose, and the barriers that keep you trapped and unable to move forward. While you are aware of certain things, much more lies beyond the immediate reach of consciousness. In order to enjoy an extraordinary life, one must learn to reprogram the subconscious.

The first thing we can do is take an honest look at ourselves. A simple analysis of the current situation we are in, but also what brought us to this point. This way we will know what we have to do so that what we manifest in the future is what we really wish to experience. If you could look at yourself from somewhere outside as if you were looking at a painting or a movie that you are not part of, without getting emotionally involved and looking at everything detached and from a different perspective, you could see everything much more clearly. Sometimes we do not allow ourselves to see things as they really are and we think we are in some way, but in reality we are very far from what we think we are.

It is said that reality does not exist unless we observe it. Also, it is shaped by our perception, and defined by our level of understanding. Your reality and what your mind can perceive cannot be the same as that of others. Your reality is yours and yours alone. What we see does not depend so much on what is in front of us, but on what we assume when we look. The eyes can look at something, but what you really see is nothing more than the perception you have of that thing. You do not see this world through your eyes, but your heart. Regardless of the impression you might have about the world, you should consider this first of all.

If you watch a campfire, you might be tormented by the thought of what might happen if it got out of control, by the fear of getting burned, or by the bad smell your clothes will carry. Or you could enjoy the warmth it gives off, be mesmerized by the beautiful, vibrant colors, and embrace the calm it brings. Similarly, when you see a child running around full of energy, you might find them noisy and irritating, or you could let their joy uplift you and fill you with energy.

In a simple black and white painting, my older sister and I saw different faces. What we noticed first wasn't just art but a reflection of ourselves. I saw an old man lost in thought, while she saw a lady turned away in silence. Where I found wisdom, she found mystery. Where I looked inward, she looked outward. Perception isn't just what we see but more about who we are. While I tend to seek meaning and look inward, she is drawn to beauty and naturally attuned to the world around her. This reminds me how beautifully each human being was created, each of us seeing the world through a different window, yet sharing the same light. Now, the question is: are you immersed in light or in darkness?

It all depends on the perspective from which you look at things. There is no such thing as good or bad. We label them as such based on how we interpret them and the type of emotion associated with those thoughts. What is good for me may not be good for you. That is why it is preferable not to judge anyone and to respect each other's point of view. We think that the eyes are the ones who see, but if two people look at the same thing, they will see everything in a very different way because the image of that thing is also influenced by how we feel. What we see is not only what we perceive with our eyes, but also according to our mood and what we have harbored deep within our being.

William Blake's statement stands as a timeless truth for the contemplative mind, holding a spiritual treasure for those who grasp its meaning: "What seems to be, is, to those to whom it seems to be." Our perception of reality also depends a lot on what we say to ourselves. Life is the way it is because that's how you see it. If you see it as a constant struggle, if you think things are hard to achieve, then that's how it will be for you. You must be aware that you are the one who creates the reality in which you actually live. Your life experiences are in line with your beliefs about life and the mindset you have. The moment you notice that things have begun to change, it will not be because they have really changed, but because you have changed the way you look at them. Once you change, the things around you will seem completely different.

In my research, I came across a recording of Bob Proctor speaking, and something he said really stuck with me. I cannot remember the exact words, but the message was clear: if we want to change our reality, we should start by changing our words. Words shape the mind. Proper management of words is of the utmost importance, because they turn into thoughts, and then into decisions. Our thoughts reveal what is going on in our minds, and the way we feel shows what is going on in our hearts. Together, these two dictate how we behave and define our personality. Our actions are shaped by how we operate and the mindset we hold. If we want to change the way we act and the results we get, we have to start by changing the way we think and feel.

Most of us live like ignorant people and some spend their entire lives without even noticing this. Where you are now and what you are experiencing is strictly determined by your faith or fear. A belief can have a negative or a positive outcome, depending on its nature. The joys and sorrows that manifest in your life are closely related to what you believe and what you take as real. The thoughts and vision you have of the things around you, through belief, you bring them to life. All that keeps you away from the life you want to live are your limited beliefs and because instead of focusing on success, you focus on failure. Instead of focusing on the solution, you focus on the problem.

Excess is bad in both ways, whether good or bad. You won't be able to enjoy the good times if you've never had bad times, because you won't know the difference between the two. A touch of negativity, doubt, or skepticism is vital, because it helps us to stay vigilant and keep ourselves safe, but be mindful not to allow it to take control over your life. You must choose to focus on the things you cherish and wish to experience.

What can you do if all that comes to your mind are endless negative thoughts that flow like a river? You think that you have no power to control what comes, but if you pay enough attention you will notice that most of them are repetitive. Predominant thoughts are the ones we focus our attention on. It is necessary to become aware and notice those moments when we channel our energy in a certain direction, regardless of whether we believe that this thing benefits or harms us.

The first step in reprogramming ourselves is to take a close look at the repetitive thoughts we have throughout the day and how they make us feel. Filter your thoughts and focus on those that bring you peace, that motivate and encourage you, that bring you closer to those passions and dreams. When you face a problem, talk about things that bring you joy or imagine positive events that could increase your happiness instead of focusing on negative feelings. Create a routine and spend a few minutes reflecting on the thoughts you have and once you identify the negative ones, simply divert yourself from them with intention and replace them with constructive ones. If you nourish your subconscious in this way, everything that comes will be a pure blessing.

Even though we can multitask, we cannot fully focus on two different things at the same time and the results will depend on our involvement. Being mindful of what you focus your attention on is crucial, as not only determination but also focus are essential on the road to success. The most influential entrepreneurs on the planet attribute much of their success to their power of focus and their ability to maintain deep focus on their vision and goals. Andrew Carnegie, one of the most influential businessmen in history, emphasized the power of focused thought and clear vision, principles that later inspired concepts like meditation, visualization, and their benefits.

There's a story often told about Andrew Carnegie that highlights just how powerful focused attention can be. Whether it's historically accurate or not, the principle still holds true. He believed we should focus our attention on a task or activity for at least five minutes without distraction. Mental discipline is nothing but a tool that helps you succeed. If the mind wanders, simply bring it back and continue the practice. This is a powerful technique, and if you put it into practice often enough, you will notice that you will do it with much more ease. Your ability to concentrate will improve, and you will become far more productive in much less time.

One day, I was traveling by metro in Valencia and I was taken by surprise when a tear ran down my cheek. I always had my headphones in, wherever I went and whatever I did, listening to my favorite music until the day I realized that it was not doing me any good. I had a song by a Spanish singer playing in my headphones, a divine voice, but such a sad song. It made me realize that the lyrics of the song I was listening to were hurting me a lot. It made me see everything I didn't have and it filled me with sadness. I realized that I was attracting all of this to me, all of the tears, all of the circumstances, and the lack of love that I felt because that's what I was thinking about all the time. Love was the most important thing to me, but instead of thinking about what would make me happy, I was only thinking about what wouldn't. When you think about or remember what happened in your past, it's like reliving the same experience in a continuous loop, instead of letting go of the discomfort it caused you at the time. In this way, your feelings of sadness and disappointment intensify.

Building on what I mentioned earlier, the choice of words is of utmost importance. In the book *The Secret* by Rhonda Byrne, I read a phenomenal example that will help you understand exactly what I mean: "To lose weight, don't focus on 'losing weight'. Instead, focus on your perfect weight." There is a big difference between the two, even though they may seem like the same thing. You want things to change, but what you are sending out is a wrong message. The Universe will not bring you what you desire, but rather the thing you focus on. If your reality is a reflection of your inner world, what are the ideas and thoughts that predominate on a regular basis? If your thoughts are filled with regret, sadness, and betrayal, you will continue to experience more of the same. You communicate with the Universe or this invisible force through emotions. You will not receive what you want, but what you focus your attention on. If you wait for your emotional state to change for the better or to feel differently in order to then initiate positive thoughts, you need to know that this will not happen. You will begin to feel differently once you start thinking differently. When you start focusing your attention on positive thoughts, such as love, kindness, respect, trust, and harmony, everything begins to change for the better and the way you feel will change.

To achieve this, one must first identify and understand the underlying reasons behind these emotions in order to improve or release them. The quality of thoughts directly influences the way we experience life. The mind gives power to anything we focus our attention on and more than that, we are the ones who create our tomorrow, through the power of thought. There are people gifted with the power to see what is going to happen in the future or there are people empowered to create the future. Both come from the same direction, depending on how we interpret it. I will tell you what will happen today. Immediately after, you will think that I am able to read the future, but what I am actually doing is creating it.

When you live in the present moment, you consciously elevate yourself, naturally rising higher and higher as you go. You will receive divine guidance to make wise decisions on the path to paradise as you recognize that you have unlimited potential to become all that you desire deep down in your soul. Regularly focus your attention on beliefs rooted in harmony, peace, and love so you will be led to a happy, abundant, and fulfilled life.

I recommend that for a few days, or as long as you think you should, analyze every thought that comes to you repetitively throughout the day. Whether they are positive or negative thoughts, take a notebook and a pen and try to write them down. This way, you can more easily identify them, uncover the beliefs hidden behind these thoughts, and begin to transform them. Take every negative thought and try to figure out where it comes from. This exercise seems a bit trivial, but all you will actually do is change your perception of something that has been imprinted in your mind and reprogram yourself. Allow yourself to see the good side in everything that surrounds you. Once you choose to do this and begin to see and accept them, you will have a completely different perception and things will not seem so bleak anymore. The way we perceive situations and respond to circumstances is deeply influenced by our attitude and mindset. The ones who are able to see the good in everything and have an attitude of gratitude toward life are more than blessed, because they know that life happens for them and not the other way around.

There are certain things we take from others, but there is a calling within each of us that is unique and comes from the unknown. We can all feel it, but how it manifests is shaped by both heredity and environment, which also influence how we interpret and respond to that inner calling. While our experiences and environment greatly influence certain personality traits, temperament and cognitive ability can be largely inherited. Heredity plays a major role in defining our personality, while our upbringing and experiences shape how it expresses itself. Though genetics and environmental factors lay the foundation, it is our perspective, habits, and daily decisions that truly define our path and who we ultimately become.

I believe that our genetic makeup can influence certain traits, interests, or preferences that mirror those of our ancestors, even without shared experiences, as they are passed down through generations. In my case, this manifests as a strong need to have everything very well organized and to be an excessively meticulous person like my grandmother. It could also be my love for gastronomy or my passion for cars, much like my father.

On the other hand, our environment plays a significant role in shaping our behavior and habits. While genes lay the foundation for our behavior, environmental factors determine how it develops and evolves. An example would be that throughout the day, every time my stepfather entered the kitchen, he would stand in front of the refrigerator, open it, look inside, then close the door and leave. It was a habit he had, without necessarily needing to consume anything, and I did the exact same thing. The funny thing is I didn't even realize this until one day when my mother was there and said: "Like father, so is the daughter." Only then was I able to notice and be aware of it. There are many things that we do on autopilot and we are not even aware of them. Imagine how many other things you do throughout the day unconsciously and that are probably not so harmless.

How are these habits formed and how can we get rid of those that do not bring us anything good? Well, there are certain things that without realizing it we end up doing repeatedly, and over time, they end up turning into habits. In order to be able to eliminate them, first of all we must be aware of them. Regular self-assessment is essential to recognize and change habits that hinder personal and professional growth. For example, I have the habit of reflecting on my actions, attitude, and behavior every day before I go to bed, in order to identify the areas in which I need to improve.

So, one day, as I was reflecting on my habits, I was about to set my alarm for the next day, and I realized that this was one of the things that was bothering me about my behavior. I was the kind of person who set no more and no less than five alarms. I was afraid that if I didn't do it, I would risk not waking up on time, because I was unconsciously cancelling the alarm. I had to change that, but how can you get rid of a bad habit, unless you replace it with a good one instead? Well, I had found the solution. I think it's been more than four years since then and today I don't have any problem. In fact, I often wake up before the alarm goes off. All I did was choose to do something that would motivate me to wake up on time, namely, to call my grandmother every day right after I wake up. It's that simple. Just find what works best for you and you'll break free from a variety of bad habits.

We have the ability to create new behavioral patterns. The trick lies in modifying small details and habits that are useless. The result will not be immediate and most likely in the first days it will be difficult for you to notice any change, but with a little patience and perseverance you will see how everything will take an unexpected turn. The circumstances of your life will change and opportunities and events will present themselves to you, which you could not have imagined. Constant repetition of the same action leads to habit formation and the more often that action is performed, the faster it will form.

And while we're on the subject of repetition, I want to mention a small, extremely important detail that made a difference in my case and will certainly do the same for you. Even after his passing, Bob Proctor continues to be one of the greatest mentors and speakers of all time, having a profound impact on an impressive number of lives and to whom millions of people, including myself, are deeply grateful. I was twenty-six when I first came across Bob's material, the same age he was in 1961 when his first mentor, Raymond Douglas Stanford, gave him Napoleon Hill's famous book, *Think and Grow Rich*, which completely transformed his life and which he studied every day until the end of his life. I've heard him mention this with so much enthusiasm countless times, and I think the reason he did it was to emphasize the impact and power of this powerful tool called repetition.

When I discovered Bob's material, it was so mesmerizing and I enjoyed listening to it so much that I made a habit of listening to one of his recordings every day while I was making dinner. My life began to change drastically, and I didn't realize what was happening until the day I heard him talk about Earl Nightingale's recordings and the impact that listening to those records over and over again had on him. It took him almost a decade to figure out what had actually happened and how through the power of repetition he had come to shift his paradigm, and then he dedicated the rest of his life to studying and teaching others to do the same.

How do you spend your days? Do the stories you hear daily align with the life you're striving for? Do they uplift you or hold you back? Are you using your time wisely? What is it that you truly want? Take a moment to reflect and answer these questions.

CHAPTER 5

God will bless your kindness and everything that you give to others, out of love, will make its way back to you, but multiplied.

Stepping Toward the Light

"Only the wise man, only he whose thoughts are controlled and purified, makes the winds and the storms of the soul obey him."

– James Allen, As a Man Thinketh

We are constantly in tune with the world around us. Whether consciously or unconsciously, every thought, emotion, and energy influences us in subtle ways, shaping our overall experience. The more aware we become of this connection, the more we can align ourselves with the Universe.

Are there more favorable or unfavorable events happening in your life? Look around you and notice that all you get is who you are rather than what you want. The reason we often struggle to attain what we desire is that we are operating on a different frequency than those things, making them inaccessible no matter how hard we try. We may not be aligned with them because we subconsciously believe we don't deserve them, or because they exist at a level beyond where we currently are. To experience them fully, we must first elevate ourselves to that level. In other words, true transformation begins with changing our way of thinking and being.

Our understanding is limited by our level of awareness. Each person operates at a unique stage of consciousness, shaped by their experiences and personal growth. Since human beings exist at different levels of consciousness, we cannot fully grasp what lies beyond our current state until we reach it, despite our common existence. This is why we sometimes do not understand others, because their reality is one we have yet to live in order to truly comprehend them. Just like climbing a mountain, our perspective is limited to the level we have reached, and as we elevate our awareness, we begin to observe what was once beyond our reach.

We are always in alignment with the flow of the Universe, which responds in harmony with our hearts. When we seek goodness, the Universe conspires to support and manifest it. When we dwell in negativity, the opposite unfolds. What you expect, will manifest. Trust your heart, as it will always guide you in the right direction.

As I mentioned in the third chapter, in the end, it turned out that leaving did not seem to be a very inspired decision for me either. Overwhelmed by thoughts, I decided to go for a walk to put them in order and clear my head. It was somewhere around ten o'clock in the evening, but I felt the need to hear my mother, although I was not going to say anything in particular. As we all know, it is almost impossible to dissimulate in front of a mother. It is as if she is always aware of everything that happens when it comes to her child. She knew something was wrong, even though she was thousands of miles away and she told me that whatever was causing me suffering, I had to leave it behind and think about what I really wanted and what would make me happy and then follow that path. Right after I hung up the call, I sat down on a bench trying my best to hold back my tears and the only thing that crossed my mind was peace. I wanted to live in peace and harmony with myself but more than that, I longed to be loved.

Make the decision about what you really want. You may think you have to do this and that or act in one way or another, and so on, but once you've made up your mind, life will set you in motion and will position you exactly where you want to go. I was convinced that I would find my way once I got there and that I would get answers to my questions and I was right, but not in the way I had imagined it would happen. It is not your job to know how to do a certain thing, but to decide to do it and then the answer will come by itself and you will find the way to get there.

After about three months, I once again decided to reorient my direction and chose to move to the UK, where my older sister had already settled and where I have been living since then. I don't think it had been a week since I arrived and I received a message from my friend, with whom I had lived for the first two weeks. She wrote that the students had returned to school and that the mother of the student to whom I had handed a CV had tried to contact me all summer, unfortunately without success. I had distributed a series of CVs throughout the center of Valencia without realizing that I had changed my contact number a few days after I had created the document, due to the low signal. I instantly knew I was exactly where I was meant to be. Perhaps I would have remained if they had reached me before my departure. But now, I can only wonder. I believe there was a calling, something beyond reason. Blessings sometimes come in disguise. You have to be patient and you will see how the lights will turn on along your path, guiding you as you go. Many times, something that seems like a misfortune can actually have unexpected benefits.

Good things come in everyone's way, but those who are truly blessed are those who especially seek to be so. I see blessings as the image of the sun. Shining freely at noon for everyone but becoming more selective in the afternoon, warming and illuminating only those who choose to seek it. For they will always find the good, even in the midst of struggle. That's why the afternoon remains my favorite time of day. The night holds its own magic, as mysteries arise from its depths, while the morning marks the beginning of a new chapter.

I have had many fortunate experiences in my life and I have learned to fully appreciate them and express my gratitude for each and every one of them every day, which has allowed me to enter and live in paradise. The secret to living a full life is to be able to look around you with love and see the good in everything and everyone. Fill your heart with gratitude. This life is a gift that many waste. Make sure you notice and are grateful for everything that surrounds you. Simply by appreciating the little things, you are heading toward a time when you will be truly grateful and you will be inclined to allow tears of joy and appreciation to flow as you let yourself be enveloped by all the magic that surrounds you.

Remember that it is absolutely impossible to be grateful and dissatisfied at the same time. Discontented people tend to focus more on the bad things than the good ones, which makes it difficult for them to find things to be grateful for. I'm not saying that I'm always one hundred percent positive, no one is. There are days when my mood dips as well, but as soon as I notice, I make an effort to shift it.

Practicing gratitude can help you change the way you feel and rise above all your discontents. Ask yourself, how am I feeling today? This simple question will help you consciously identify your current state. Develop an attitude of gratitude and shift your mindset by focusing on the good things as much as you can and always look for the positive side in everything. Since I was a child, I've learned from my grandmother to have faith in God and to cultivate an attitude of gratitude. She always counts her blessings and expresses gratitude for what she has accomplished at the end of each day. The more you practice gratitude, the more reasons you will have to be grateful. By cultivating gratitude every day, you will generate a great impact. There will always be room for more to be grateful for, because we will never be able to give as much as we receive.

When I was little, I went to a church and there was a pastor who, when he prayed, did it in a very different way from the others, and I had never seen anyone else do it before him. His body would simulate a friendly hug, with his arms open to the sky, as if he were waiting for the rain to touch his palms. It took me a few years to understand what he was actually doing, and later I heard some great mentors talk about it at some point. It's like you open your heart to absolutely everything, enveloped in serenity and unable to resist anything. In all splendor, calm and patient, you open yourself to possibility, ready to receive all that is good and all that is miraculous: God's blessing.

By talking about blessings, you begin to realize that when you stop searching for the right person, that's exactly when they will enter your life. The truth is that I was firmly convinced that sooner or later this person would appear in my life, and I decided that in the meantime I would do everything to become a better person and find the favorable means to achieve what I set out to do, so all I did was focus my attention on this. That person I had been searching for had suddenly arrived and I didn't even have time to assimilate everything that was happening around me. The moment he appeared, I recognized him as the one I had always been waiting for, because I already had a clear image of how this person would be, the one with whom I would choose to stay with for the rest of my life.

In the previous chapter I mentioned that moment in the subway precisely with the intention of making you understand how important what we say to ourselves is, more specifically the words and impressions we have, and how all of these consequently attract everything that surrounds us. The night before my subway ride was when I watched the famous documentary *The Secret* by Rhonda Byrne. Although I had heard about it four years after its release, from the professor I mentioned in the second chapter, it had been twelve years before I finally watched it. I had just been too busy to make time for it, but if you ask me now, I really don't know what I was busy with. The suffering and emptiness I felt in my soul made me look in my past, to cling to every good thing I had experienced, and that's how I remembered that moment in the high school locker room. All those testimonies from the documentary changed the way I perceived life and it is intriguing that today, there are still people who have not heard of it.

From that day on, I refused to think about all the things that bothered me in my previous relationships, everything that did not match my expectations and desires, and everything that hurt me and made me drift away. I created a list of small details that built the perfect image of the partner that I would have considered ideal for me, then imagined and visualized our meetings and how the day would have gone for us, what our actions and conversations would have been, including his attitude and character.

It is often said that Albert Einstein believed that everything is energy. Everything in the universe is made of energy and vibrates at a specific frequency. What we receive is simply a reflection of the energy we generate and the vibration we emit into the universe. The key to manifesting what you desire is aligning your frequency with that of what you want. Bob Proctor has created an insightful lesson available online, where he explains the law of vibration, which is considered the foundation of the law of attraction. According to him, this is one of the most fundamental laws of the universe, and I wholeheartedly recommend you check it out. Sandy Gallagher, Bob Proctor's business partner, friend, and co-founder of the Proctor Gallagher Institute, wrote an article called "Seven Universal Laws at a Glance" in which I found this sentence that says everything you need to understand: "There is a connection between your feelings, what you attract to yourself, and the results you get in your life."

Every human being has a unique definition of love, and most of us claim that it would be a mixture of various feelings specific to each of us. But what is love truly? Well, this question cannot be answered with certainty, but I will share with you what love truly means to me. You might be among those who will say that love is often painful and that most of us end up suffering because of love, but that feeling you are talking about could be anything but love. Love could mean so many things to some and so little to others. There are those who will say that over time this feeling fades, until eventually it disappears. That cannot be true at all, unless we are referring to anything but love. Love is the nature of our being and will last forever, because it has always been there. It is already there, within us, we just have to allow it to be and express itself freely.

Love is the highest form of energy and the most powerful force in the vast universe. It vibrates at a frequency higher than any other type of energy, making it the most elevated form of energy both on Earth and throughout the universe. Love connects us to the highest energetic frequency, guiding us closer to our true selves. Its vibration lifts us to a higher state of consciousness, dissolving negativity and freeing us from any burdens.

I used to think that I understood everything about love or that I already knew what it was, but the truth is I had no idea before I met my fiancé. This feeling of pure serenity, that mixture of peace, harmony, and calm, I had never experienced it before.

That absence of fear, uncertainty, and anxiety. I used to think that love brings happiness, but that it also comes with suffering. I think most people think that way and I was one of them too. I used to believe that in order to be loved, you had to fight and make all sorts of compromises, yet even then, it never seemed to work.

Like me, there are so many people who have misunderstood and even suffer for it, because they don't understand where they are wrong. You have to understand only one thing: love does not ask for anything, it simply is. Everything else is called attachment rather than love. Love is often confused with attachment, which is why there are people who tend to think they are in love or that they love someone, but in reality they are attached to them as someone can become attached to their home or to certain objects that keep their memories alive. Perhaps now you will wonder if it is possible to love someone, but at the same time also be attached to them. The answer is yes. Even being aware of this, it is almost impossible for a human being to separate the two. I believe only a small number of people can truly distinguish between the two and perceive them separately. When you love someone, you naturally want that person by your side. However, if the love isn't mutual, it becomes difficult for the emotionally involved person to move forward, especially if they can't differentiate between the two. In most cases, the only way to heal is by finding a new love.

I see life as a journey, like a cruise. Of course, I want to enjoy the ride and create a set of precious memories. So, if there is something that bothers me, thoughts that disturb me or make me feel uncomfortable, I choose not to go. When choosing a partner, keep this in mind and the fact that most of the time you should feel joy rather than sadness. If you feel that the person you are with at the moment is harming you more than bringing you joy, then you need to let go. This continuous struggle of back and forth and uncertainty does nothing but make us sick.

You will instantly connect with your soulmate and you will light up as soon as your paths cross. You will experience a strong connection and a sense of familiarity, as if you already know them, and your relationship will be intense and meaningful from the beginning. You will know immediately because, as if by magic, it will elevate your soul. This seems to be the perfect time for every human being, the one in which we will find that divine connection between ourselves and another human being. We are made of love, but what we call love between two people is more of a unique bond, a moment when two souls resonate and vibrate in unison. But more than that, it is tolerance, understanding, and goodwill toward the other.

Soulmates are formed when two kindred souls recognize each other and naturally complement one another, because they share similar values. It's as if they were one soul, separated to live in two different bodies. Mutual love is what happens when someone appears and helps sustain and uplift the other. As soon as they get closer to each other, a circle full of light is formed, enveloping them completely. Simply being aware of this wonderful encounter could be the beginning of a life full of happiness for both of them, enjoying peace and great achievements.

The people we admire and feel drawn to are often those who resonate at a higher frequency than we do. We attract individuals who are similar to us, those with whom we share a resonance. While we may be attracted to people with a higher energy level, we are more likely to form relationships with those who vibrate at the same frequency as ourselves. We can only attract what aligns with our own energy. Often, these relationships don't work because what we truly want isn't always what we end up attracting. It's important to understand that the people who come into our lives do so because their energy matches our own. This is why we sometimes feel as though we've attracted the same person in a different body. What we attract is in harmony with who we are, and no matter how perfect our ideal may seem, we can only achieve it if we are willing to change.

We can truly attract the energy we desire by rising to a higher level than where we currently are. The world is constantly evolving, changing, and expanding, and so are we. To fulfill your desires, you must become the energy you wish to attract into your life. We need to learn to embody that energy ourselves so it can return to us. Cultivating inner balance, gratitude, and love is key to reaching a higher energy frequency.

What does happiness look like and how does it manifest itself? It's not those intense moments when your heart beats extremely fast, but rather the natural state of being at peace and a continuous feeling of contentment and gratitude.

If you are not happy, then you will look for people, things, and reasons to keep you busy and all your attention will be directed toward ways and means to satisfy your personal needs. All action and energy will revolve around you. When you are truly happy, everything flows naturally as you seek to fulfill your desires and enhance the happiness of those around you. Life becomes more about others and how we can contribute to their well-being.

How would you describe happiness? I find it in simple things. Nothing grandiose, just the simple fact of being and feeling at peace. I remember one day, when I was about seven or eight years old, I went for a walk with my stepfather and on the way we were approached by different types of people. No matter who that person was with whom he came into contact, he always respectfully greeted them and pronounced their names. Have you noticed how involved the other person becomes in an interaction when their name is invoked? It works like a magic wand to capture anyone's attention. Well, at one point, while a man was heading toward us, my stepfather put his hands on my shoulders saying with enthusiasm and with the widest smile possible: "This is my daughter, Cosmina," after which he proposed to stop by a store on the way home to buy pretzels and peanuts.

It was an extraordinary day, in which I plunged into an ocean of happiness and I can say that this is one of the many childhood memories that I love the most, such as the Saturdays spent at my grandmother's house or the barbecues organized by my biological father on the river bank and where I always had such a great time with my wonderful sisters. Going back to the day in question, what he did was make me feel important, loved, and appreciated. Often, as adults we overlook these small details in all this rush, but children are much more receptive and that was a valuable lesson for me, although he was probably not aware of what he had done. You don't have to do impressive things or move mountains for your children, but be there to support them when they need you and bring them joy.

Another thing to mention would be that as human beings we have this need for connection, to be seen and appreciated. I noticed this repeatedly in both my grandmother and my stepfather and how the people they came across totally changed their mood. I thought it was because they always approached others with a positive attitude and then, of course, they were inevitably considered pleasant company. However, what they did was show those people that they cared, made them feel appreciated, and enhanced the idea that what the other had to say and offer was valuable. Let others see and feel how important they are to you, and treat them the way you would like others to treat you. In an attempt to make them feel better after their encounter with you, you will always be respected and welcome wherever you go.

When you give something to someone, give it wholeheartedly. Do it whenever you can and not just when you see someone at an impasse. We are so used to listing everything we give, nothing we receive in return. When you help someone, don't just do it because you are asked to do so, but because you want to. Never expect anything in return and even more than that, never remind those people again and again how much you have given them and how much you have helped them. Better choose not to give anything this way, rather than complain about it later. If the lack and need are at the base of the act, then the chances that what you will attract in return is of the same nature are enormous. If you knew that abundance flows infinitely, nothing would stop you.

Give whenever you think you can do it and do it with a pure thought and an open heart. Otherwise, you will not bring any benefit to anyone, neither to the other nor to yourself. Be a light to them. Be the kind of person who lights up the lives of others, lighting their way and making things easier for them. I absolutely love this quote by Ludwig van Beethoven, as cited in *Beethoven: The Creator* by Romain Rolland: "I recognize no sign of superiority in mankind other than goodness." God will bless your kindness and everything that you give to others, out of love, will make its way back to you, but multiplied. Because there is no one else to give, but yourself. The moment you understand this, you will have found the solution to all your problems.

When I lived in Spain a decade ago, I was taking care of the elderly, and I met a charming man whose age was almost a century old. Every morning he sipped his coffee along with a piece of toast with olive oil. As a rule, he would leave a small piece of bread reserved for birds on his plate and asked me: "Did you remember to give them something today?" If you left the kitchen door open, you could see the terrace directly from the living room. As soon as I put the bread out for the birds, I would sit in the lounge in the armchair next to him and watch him. I did it every day and it was my favorite moment of the morning, waiting to see his reaction. An immensity of things were lying in his eyes. It could easily have gone unnoticed, but not if you paid enough attention. It wasn't just the joy itself of watching the birds peck, it was as if the entire universe began to shine and bloom in his eyes, just through the simplicity of giving those crumbs to other creatures.

That's when I understood what love is, and I don't just mean love toward another person, but toward the entire creation. This is what is called divine grace. Harmony, peace, and happiness placed in an embrace that encompasses everything and that in the rush, we barely notice. Now I know that what you give is so little compared to what you receive, but if you do it, it is as if you have the power to give life. By contributing to it, you are equally part of creation.

CHAPTER 6

Turn your face toward the sun so you can see Heaven is exactly where you have always been.

Hell Vs. Heaven

"He who lives in harmony with himself lives in harmony with the universe."

– Marcus Aurelius Antoninus, *Meditations*

Have you ever wondered if Heaven and Hell aren't places, but rather states of being? A description of how you look on the inside that is then projected onto the outside. And what if the "judgment" takes place here on Earth, in day-to-day life?

Don't be afraid when your life starts to fall apart, that means it's working. The Universe is creating space for your desires. Recognizing your innate power is the first step toward achieving your goals. Cultivate well-being and serenity as your natural state of mind. When you embrace peace fully, nothing can shake you, and the path to happiness and true bliss will unfold before you. Turn your face to the sun so you can see Heaven is right in front of you and where you have always been. If you can't see it through your eyes, open your heart so you can feel it.

We can say that if each of us has a distinct perspective on the world, then it would be as if we all lived in different worlds from each other. No matter how hard we try, we can never fully understand or observe another person's point of view because each person sees as they are. But I can assure you that this is true for each of us, that if we let our heart open, we have automatically stepped into paradise. And when I say this, I do not mean that place bathed in pure bliss, that realm of blessings and eternal life located somewhere in the clouds, where they say we will go after death, but a state of being, here on Earth.

When I was around ten years old, I was coming back from school and on the way home I saw a gentleman in a drunken state, who dropped a banknote, about five pounds in today's times. My first thought was to warn him, but after observing him more closely, I decided not to return the money, thinking that I was doing him a favor. As a child, I always kept what I received for special occasions, so my parents didn't find anything suspicious when I returned home with a bag full of snacks, which I placed under the Christmas tree. Right after the holidays, my mother sent me shopping, and when I got home, I was missing exactly the amount of money I had wrongfully taken that day. The worst part was that I hadn't lost my own savings, but my family's.

Do not touch anything that does not belong to you, because sooner or later the payment will be made in one way or another. Whatever you give, you will receive, and whatever you take, it will be taken from you. Maybe not in the same way, but with the same energy. That day I learned not only that it is not good to take something that does not belong to you, but that we are not in a position to judge anyone, because in the end we do not know what is in anyone's heart. Moreover, don't dictate to anyone what to do and don't force anyone to change; they will do it when they feel they want to do so or when they feel ready for it. All we can do is advise and support the other, but nothing more, the rest is up to each one.

Unexpressed emotions can generate anxiety. Those who often tend to hide their emotions may end up suffering from anxiety, experience panic attacks, or even become depressed. Depression is often caused by a mixture of factors, and emotional suppression can be one of them. Keeping track of your emotions can help release a good amount of tension that has been stored inside you. It is essential to release any emotions that keep your body tense. If you find it difficult to manage your emotions, an underlying imbalance may be the cause. When you cultivate inner peace and embrace yourself unconditionally, you naturally activate a state of overall harmony.

Most people who don't like themselves hate being alone and spend most of their time in the company of other people. They always feel the need to distract themselves from their own thoughts and are often frustrated and dissatisfied. Another aspect would be honesty. When you start hiding things or having secrets, it is simply because you are ashamed of your actions. This should be the first signal that what you are doing is wrong. We must take responsibility for our actions regardless of the circumstances, both toward ourselves and toward others. Growth and improvement are part of life, and you are constantly evolving. You can become the person you want to be, but you have to make an effort.

You have a choice and you are free to choose. Being yourself means expressing your authentic self, regardless of external pressures. Are you truly honest with yourself? The real you is that version of you when no one else is present and when you are completely alone. Those who are transparent with themselves live their lives according to their true values and, because of their energy, we can see them shining from afar. Authentic people are not just who they appear to be, but who they really are.

Integrity is the cornerstone of a person's character, often regarded as one of the most essential and defining qualities one can embody. One of the most important questions you should ever ask yourself is: who are you as a person? You must be aware of who you are, understand your attitude toward life, and act in alignment with that understanding. If you don't like what you see, then you need to change those things. Otherwise, you will face the same problems over and over again, endlessly.

"I don't do it because I don't get paid enough for it." I hear people say this every day. If there's one thing I've learned, it's that you always, always have to give your all, at all times and regardless of what you get in return. Those who truly care will notice. You have to give your all, as if you're doing it for no one else but yourself. That way, you'll enjoy your work no matter the circumstances. Ask yourself: "Does what I am about to do bring me joy?" Then go for it, but if not, then find a way to stop doing it. If for any reason it is a must, then try changing the way you complete the task by taking a different approach to it. Once you are and act this way, the results will be impressive, you will be appreciated, and eventually you will receive your reward.

Take full responsibility for the quality of your life. Everything you experience at the moment that doesn't go according to your expectations is because you don't really know what you want. Because you haven't made up your mind yet and because you've mostly never made decisions on your own and you've always felt the need to be guided by others in every aspect of your life. To gain a deeper understanding of your needs, feelings, and desires, take time for introspection.

Get rid of all those accumulations that don't define you and start from scratch. From the beginning, as if you were about to fully create your character in a video game, but this time, you will be the piece you've got to work on. Without second thoughts, without excuses, and with a bit of dedication, you will be able to reshape yourself entirely. With the right mindset, amazing things will be within your reach. You will notice that small daily efforts dedicated to improvement will produce incredibly positive results. Just like in a video game, you have the ability to create your character exactly the way you want it to be and on top of that, you can improve it at any time. Leave the things that no longer serve you or that don't fit the person you want to become and create new ones. If you commit to yourself, you have the power to create remarkable things.

The future is uncertain and so the idea that the plans we make can get out of control scares us, which is why most people avoid making plans for the future and live spontaneously. I like to make plans for the future and I believe that the most efficient and successful people are those who organize and manage their time efficiently. I'm not saying that being spontaneous is bad, on the contrary, I think it's necessary to dedicate part of the time to venture and embrace the unknown, but those who manage to enjoy a good life are those who pay special attention to detail, plan everything very carefully, and this way they are able to create and attract extraordinary things in their life. Also, I consider that by knowing what's coming next, it could help you reduce worries about the unknown and be more present in the moment.

Another way to help prevent feeling overwhelmed is to maintain a clear, clean, and organized space in your home or in the places where you spend most of your time. Get rid of things that no longer serve you and display the things that inspire you the most and that bring you peace and joy, without overloading the space. Organizing your home will provide you with a more efficient living environment and help you feel more in control of your space and daily activities, also reducing stress, improving mental clarity, and increasing productivity.

We are what we consume, both physically and mentally, and to some extent, we are shaped by the environment that surrounds us. That said, a good diet and proper rest also play a crucial role in our overall well-being. Are you aware that the content you engage in programs your subconscious according to the words you listen to repeatedly and not only that, but the emotions they arouse in you? I never liked listening to the news and every time it was projected into the space I was in, I disappeared. We are not aware of the impact the things we feed our bodies and minds with have on us, otherwise we would be much more careful about what we do.

Surround yourself with the right people, those who are at peace with themselves, who have a positive attitude toward life, and who focus on beautifying their soul. You will be surprised by the way one person communicates with another or in which direction the discussion goes, when they are in the right company or vice versa. It's so important who you spend time with and what speech you pay attention to, no matter how trivial that sounds. I once heard someone say that if you're in a group where everyone gives you a compliment, but you only remember the one person who didn't, it reveals that your mindset may be trapped in negativity. That's why it's important to surround yourself with people who have a positive attitude, especially until you've built one for yourself. Pay close attention to those around you and how they make you feel. If someone doesn't bring any positivity into your life, try to distance yourself and limit interactions as much as possible. This is essential because otherwise, your efforts toward growth and inner peace may be in vain.

I think that the main reason for someone's inability and distrust is given by the tendency and the attempt of parents to control everything in relation to their children. When I was little, my mother was very protective of my sisters, brother, and me, yet she also gave us enough freedom in our actions and decisions. I'm sure this helped us tremendously, allowing us to grow and become independent from a very young age. Children must be allowed to make decisions on their own, otherwise they will never be fully prepared for adversity.

We grow up with the idea that we owe something to someone. We live with the preconception that life is hard and that we have to work hard to prepare our descendants with a better future, but we did not come to this world to amass fortunes, but to enjoy. Parents struggle their entire lives to give their children everything and leave them inheritances. This way, they never get to enjoy their own lives. It is so wrong to do that. Some people take out loans just to please their children, only to struggle afterward. They feel compelled to do so because their parents did it for them, just as their grandparents did before them. Even if that weren't the case, they still feel it is their duty. You don't owe your children anything, just help them grow and be there to support and love them. That's all they need and nothing more. If you have something to give, do it with all your heart, otherwise don't worry, they will find a way to manage on their own.

I don't deny that I've always seen myself as a successful, wealthy, and admirable person. That vision is what motivated me to take action, because deep down, I believed it was possible. Those who succeed often picture themselves in that position, even if they don't fully believe they can achieve it. The key is to desire it enough to begin and then invest the time needed to develop the skills to make it happen.

I had many ideas and desires to pursue all kinds of things, truly good ideas, but I often lost interest because each one was driven by the need to earn more money. To be honest, it was never as much about me as it was about my loved ones. When I was a child, I saw that those around me had many shortcomings and I promised myself that when I grew up, I would take care of all of us. I told myself that I would help them and that I would bring abundance into everyone's lives. At the time, this was the biggest dream I had, and I genuinely believed that having money meant having everything: health, success, and happiness. Now I understand that money is simply a tool that helps you enjoy life more fully. It can provide access to better healthcare, open doors to opportunities, and offer comfort, but it is not the true source of those things.

I realized that you don't need money to help others live better lives. They can do it on their own, once they apply these principles in their lives. And that's why I finally made the decision to write this book and for me there is nothing greater in this world than the idea that these lines could help someone today and even if there is only one person on this Earth who reads these lines, my intention was worth carrying out.

The luckiest and most blessed people on the planet are those who set their goals based on the needs of people, to make a difference and to benefit the world. Those who focus on serving others, making a positive impact, and contributing to the world often find that success follows naturally. The one who combines their passions and skills to create something that serves others will be the one to fulfill their own desires. Whoever manages to do this has truly discovered a treasure. In *The Strangest Secret*, Earl Nightingale shares the idea that our financial return is directly linked to the level of service we provide. This powerful concept, drawn from the wisdom of Earl Nightingale, emphasizes that the better we are at providing service and doing our work with excellence, the greater the rewards will be.

Those who think rich people are being insincere when they say money won't make you happy or fulfilled are misunderstanding the deeper truth. You can have everything you want yet still feel empty deep down. Achieving financial stability or acquiring material possessions alone won't bring true fulfillment. Why is that? Because fulfillment comes from growth. When you focus on personal development, money and everything else you desire will follow as a bonus to the many blessings already unfolding. This is the main reason why I decided to share my story with the rest of the world, with the intention to help others see the world from someone else's perspective, as one day it was very helpful to me.

When I first started writing, I had no idea where to begin. I sat in front of my laptop, staring at a blank screen with an equally blank mind. But somehow, along the way, I managed to gather my thoughts and piece them together to bring them to life. I realized that there are all kinds of thoughts and ideas that come to my mind throughout the day, so I formed the habit of carrying a pen with me everywhere I went and if for some reason I didn't have it with me, I wrote it down on my phone. This way I was able to observe my thoughts more clearly and I recommend you do the same. A journal will help you gain more clarity about what's going on in your mind. Writing down your thoughts and displaying your feelings could help you detach yourself from them, as it allows you to become aware of them.

The money, relationships, and health you have at the moment reflect your state of mind. If you want to enjoy financial freedom, a healthy love relationship, or optimal health, it is necessary to pay more attention to yourself. A mindset rooted in scarcity, constantly thinking about lack and problems, will make it impossible to embrace abundance, and all that will come your way in the future will be more lack and need. The same applies if you buy something for personal enjoyment but then feel guilty about it. The next time, you might hesitate and think, "But what if something comes up and I need this amount of money? It's better to be cautious." And guess what? Something will happen.

Everything is created from within. In the past, my friendship with money was quite shaky. When the subject of money made its way into the discussion, I felt an annoying emptiness in my stomach, because I knew I wasn't doing very well. Every time my fiancé asked me how my finances were going this month, I felt a lump in my throat. I had to pluck up the courage every time before taking a look at my bank account and that's why, most of the time, I didn't know exactly how much I had left. It is a very delicate subject for most of us, because every time you have the feeling that you have to choose between one thing or another and be mindful of what you spend. You feel a constant frustration that no matter how hard you try to earn more, it seems to somehow disappear afterward. My fiancé always knew how much he had and what he spent it on, so I thought he knew something that I didn't and maybe I needed to change the way I looked at money.

As a child, I often heard that money brings misfortune and that those who have money are certainly doing something immoral. You've probably heard similar claims that money changes a person and turns them evil once they acquire it, or that bad luck and misfortune follow those who become wealthy. But I believe that money simply amplifies your core values and reveals who you truly are. A person with strong moral principles will remain the same, even after acquiring wealth. Money is only a tool and cannot influence in any way, except to expose what that person is really like.

Furthermore, do you think that if one day you had large sums of money, all your problems would end and that you would live a perfect life? Of course not. You would run into the same problems, the money would be wasted, and you would remain exactly the same. No matter how much you win, events will unfold in such a way that you will always reach the same point, unless you decide to change in the meantime. So, one day I sat and imagined what my relationship with money would look like, if it were a person. I realized that I didn't treat it well at all and that I also had repulsive behavior toward it. How can I enjoy something or someone if I'm not willing to welcome it into my life? What is your opinion about money? To enjoy a certain thing's presence, you have to allow it to enter into your life. To feel deserving and worthy of that thing and to receive it with an open heart.

You are absolutely aware that you will forget certain things throughout your life and a large part of your memories will also be erased over time, so ask yourself these questions. Is this truly beneficial for me? Should I keep it? Is it really important for me to remember it? You are in charge and you have the power to choose what you want to remember or not. I always choose the good ones and everything else just doesn't matter to me at the end of the day, because they don't serve me any purpose so I get rid of them. This is, for me, the gateway to Heaven.

When we visualize, we're essentially creating new memories, and there are no strict rules about how we imagine our future desires in order to bring them into reality. You might think that we should see the image through the lens of our own eyes, as if experiencing it from the first person, but you can also view it as if from the third person. The first perspective involves emotional and sentimental engagement, while the second allows you to observe your attitude and personality as an outsider. From my perspective, both are equally important. This technique can help you form vivid and clear mental images, which, when combined with consistent effort and action, can ultimately bring your deepest desires into reality.

When you reflect on your memories, the reason you revisit them is often to find answers, whether to understand how you felt or to see how the situation unfolded and how you acted in that precise moment. Introspection allows you to examine your thoughts, feelings, and actions from that time, giving you a broader perspective on the entire context of the event. Take a moment to look back at the past and analyze some of your memories. Notice how they present themselves, and you will gain a deeper understanding through an analysis conducted from an external viewpoint. This practice will help you intentionally manifest your future goals and aspirations.

You have the ability to filter and organize your memories, choosing what you wish to remember and retain. When we talk about memories, the ones that bring us joy are treasures, so we keep them carefully, but there are some that we would like to forget. You have to let go of the emotions that keep you trapped in the experience of unpleasant memories. There may be some kind of event that has marked you and that makes you feel like you can't do it, but trust me when I say, you have the ability to do it. You need to begin a process of cleansing these accumulations that are no longer of any use to you and that you have held onto for years, releasing them little by little so that they dissolve. Just like removing the dry leaves of a plant, you simply let go of everything that blocks your blooming and drains your energy. The more easily you believe you can release those emotions, the quicker and smoother the process will be. As soon as they dissolve, you will feel as light as a feather. The speed of healing will depend on each person's belief and willingness to embrace the process.

Nowadays, people are not as patient as they used to be and they get agitated, upset, and angry much too quickly. People who are patient and tolerant lead less stressful lives and find it much easier to overcome certain challenges in life. The path to greatness is to develop a mindset based on faith and understanding. To live a peaceful life, it's essential to practice patience and tolerance, and to focus on the positive in all situations. By sealing yourself from negativity, nothing will truly affect you. Controlling your emotions doesn't mean detaching or suppressing your feelings, but rather strengthening yourself to remain steady in the face of challenges.

Self-control is the ability of each person to control themselves regardless of the situations that arise. Sometimes we are not ready for what is to come, but it is up to us how we react. It is not so much about what happens to us, but about how we respond or react to these events. We often tend to imagine things that did not happen on the physical plane and make thousands and thousands of disappointing scenarios that feed our subconscious in an unhealthy way and that affect us not only mentally, but physically. We hurt ourselves involuntarily and we don't realize the power of the thoughts and images we create through our conscious mind. We begin to feel this restlessness in our body, which turns into pain and slowly, slowly, we end up getting sick.

How many times have you had a heated conversation with someone and then when you were left alone you imagined all kinds of scenarios in which you added something offensive and the whole scene began to fill with aggression, even more than what really happened in reality? You're probably blaming yourself for not being more judgmental of the other person. This whole mental process does nothing more than transmit data to the Universe about what you would assume you experienced in reality. The Universe does not differentiate between what is real and what you imagine and the consequences will always be based on what you thought. Therefore, every time you get emotionally involved in any kind of action, or if you happen to have a conflict with someone, try to change that catastrophic ending with a handshake using your imagination and detach yourself with a sense of peace.

I have always preferred to act as if I knew nothing or let people think whatever they wanted, even if I thought their opinion was wrong. I like to believe that there is a process in everything and that time will tell the truth. It is not your job to explain anything to anyone and most of the time the other person is not ready to hear what you have to say anyway. If you can help someone, do so, but if your involvement will only lead to more conflict, it's better to step back. I assure you that letting go and moving on is the healthiest approach, regardless of the situation.

When I didn't like someone, I tried to get to know them better because there are things we notice in others that we don't like, but the truth is that what we see in others is a reflection of ourselves. If you try to analyze a little, you will discover a lot about yourself and then you will end up asking yourself: "Why are they criticizing me? Everything I do is good." Well, maybe because you have criticized others yourself, or maybe it's something you still have to work on, or maybe you are placed in those situations precisely with the intention of discovering something specific or becoming more understanding. Until you recognize that each of us is unique and has a different perspective on the reality we live in, you will keep encountering the same concerns. Each of us experiences life according to the perspective we adopt and the way we operate. None of us are completely similar to the other, although sometimes it seems that way. We all see things differently and the best thing we can do is not criticize. When we criticize someone, we are actually criticizing ourselves.

They are all just reflections of me. When you begin to see the other as another version of yourself, you will look at them with compassion and understanding. As you could be if you wanted to or as you shouldn't be. The moment you realize that others are just reflections of you, there will be no more envy, anger, remorse, and you will finally be free. If we pay enough attention to all the people we come into contact with, we will realize that there is a lot to learn and even from those who may have once hurt us. Once you choose and allow yourself to think this way, you will begin to see others exactly as they really are, and the reason behind their actions will not affect you as they did before.

I may be called the devil himself in the stories of some or a fallen angel in others, but this is only the fruit of their perception. Events and people often come into our lives to help us achieve something. Sometimes we even end up getting hurt on the path to truth, but if we learn something from the experience, we are blessed. Don't take anything personally and always be good and kind to those around you; we are all here to learn. Also, be understanding with yourself, don't blame yourself for things that have no other purpose than to burden you, and be patient and aware that things take time to change, but they will.

I often hear: "I hate this person, he's unbearable." Well, I believe that once you start paying closer attention and get to know that person better, you will realize you were mistaken about them. There are various reasons why they behave in one way or another. It's something that upsets them, that bothers them, or they were simply raised that way and they don't know how to be otherwise. Most of them are not even aware of their behavior and do so unconsciously. You might think that you are a good person because you often tend to help the people around you, but pay attention to the nature of your thoughts. Your inner dialogue and the thoughts that pass through your mind reveal everything about you. That is who you really are. I've often been called the devil's advocate, but I don't take sides. I simply observe what triggers people's reactions and choose to focus on their positive qualities instead.

Another vital skill is learning to listen. These days, most people are focused on making their point and being heard. We all have something to say, but very few of us truly listen. It is a beautiful thing when spoken words genuinely serve the listener, but many speak without pause, unaware of how to stop and listen the other person. Some interrupt frequently simply because they lack the patience to listen. Moreover, while someone else is speaking, they are often not truly present, but simply preparing their next response.

When you listen to something or read something, you naturally reflect on the thought that has captured your attention. Every time your focus is drawn to a particular passage, it feels like a revelation, and in that moment, you stop truly listening to what follows. If you listen to something more than once, you'll realize just how much you missed the first time. That's why I rewind and listen again and again. When we listen, we often get caught up in thinking about one specific point, and everything else that follows fades into the background. If you listen to the same recording again, you might feel as though it's your first time hearing it, because you don't remember what was said before, and you must pick up from where you left off.

The same principle applies when talking to others. You must learn to be a good listener and talk less. Often, we believe we already know what the other person will say, but more times than not, we are wrong. This is the root cause of much confusion and misunderstanding. If we want to learn something, we must first learn to listen. If you're seeking clarity in your life, listen. If you want to open your mind and grow, listen. No matter what you aim to do, you can find a faster answer or solution by remaining silent. Once you begin applying this in your life, you'll see that you can achieve results in an incredibly short amount of time.

CHAPTER 7

The one who has ever felt or become aware that there is more beyond their limited condition is consciousness itself and is ready to discover the truth.

The CREATOR

"To reach a higher level of being, you must assume a higher concept of yourself."
— Neville Goddard, *The Power of Awareness*

The moment I began to truly be myself was the moment I opened the doors to a magical realm, where I encountered everything I had been searching for throughout my entire existence. Nothing is more fulfilling than living in harmony with yourself, with your true self. Miracles will begin to unfold in your life, and you will come to realize that you have always lived in paradise. You just couldn't see it.

We often search for answers outside ourselves, clinging to all sorts of things that only deepen our confusion. The one who has ever felt or realized that there is more beyond their limited condition is consciousness itself and is ready to find out the truth. The only way to truly connect with ourselves is to look within. But how does one truly do that?

Today, as the world places so much focus on the body, I hold hope that tomorrow will center more on the soul. The deep doubts we carry about ourselves and the questions we ask about the meaning of life often arise from an identity crisis rooted in the ego. It is said that the ego is our enemy because it distorts or denies reality, while the true self accepts it. Yet, without the ego, we might not be able to experience this human journey. Today, people often feel the need to identify with all sorts of things, placing meaningless labels on themselves that have nothing to do with who they truly are. What were we before we were human?

The deeper you dive into knowledge, the more you become aware of the vastness of untapped aspects. Your awareness will grow through study, learning, and applying all of this in your daily life. All the effort you put into accumulating knowledge will be of no use to you, if you don't put those things into practice. Most of us know how to do things better, but most of the time we don't do them.

Approach every situation with confidence and consistency in thought, emotion, and action. The answers will come from within as soon as you turn your attention inward and seek inner guidance. When you realize the power you have been given, you will embark on the path to endless happiness, freedom, and peace of mind. We are more than we allow ourselves to see, and there is so much more beyond this physical body. We are spiritual beings.

I believe that the Bible is the book of life and that it comes from a deep collaboration between humanity and God. The things we find inside the Bible are more like metaphors than stories of events as we were taught. Those are secrets left in plain sight for those who are able to observe them.

The Bible says that God is the creator of all things and that we are part of creation. Moreover, that we are the highest form of creation. God is described as omnipotent (all powerful), omniscient (all knowing), and omnipresent (present everywhere at all times). God is the life force flowing through all things. So, can we say that God is the universe itself? Or I should say, energy, as scientists prefer to call it.

Initially, man was created in the image and likeness of God, but after the fall into sin, man was created in the image and likeness of the earthly. However, the center of the human being is the soul, where the power that God has given resides. The fall into sin does not represent a moral decline, but the loss of awareness of our true nature. It is a state of forgetting our divine essence. We become disconnected from the divine source within us and identify more with the earthly self, which is the ego. The way to reconnect and awaken to our true identity lies within the soul, waiting to be remembered.

I cannot claim to be a follower of any particular religion, although I have shared a few Bible insights in this book and strongly affirm my belief in the existence of God. There is a supreme power that reigns everything and everywhere and the one who can see a bridge between science and spirituality, and embrace both, is the one who manages to get answers much more easily. As I mentioned in the first chapter, I believe that we are all talking about the same thing, regardless of which side we are on or the name we give to this supreme power.

Our attitude toward life determines the outcome we experience through the power of free will. The Bible says that the destiny of each of us was already written. I believe that the decisions you make dictate the path you are on and that your story has been written in infinite possibilities, and based on what you choose is how your life will be created and unfolded. Life is nothing more than an experience of being. You identify yourself as being this mind and voice that you hear in your head, but how do you explain that you can observe those thoughts running over and over again in your mind, unless you are separate from it? Try to set aside any ideas related to personal identity, convictions, and beliefs about the world, and simply observe.

The Bible also says that people are made up of three parts: spirit, soul, and body. At the level of the body, we interact with this physical world. The soul is the core essence, the realm of decision, that establishes the identity of an individual as being the Earth suit. The spirit is the breath of life, the divine nature of the soul, and the immediate connection with God. All influence one another. The mind is like a portal to our inner dimensions, acting as a mediator between the body, soul, and spirit. Imagine the three aspects of the mind as being the heart. The conscious, the subconscious, and the superconscious represent the body, the soul, and the spirit. The temporal suit is the body, your core essence is your soul, and the spark in your soul is your spirit. The bridge between the two, physical and spiritual, realms is undoubtedly the soul. It is what creates the reality in which every human being lives.

Every human being comes into this world carrying with them this creative power capable of creating extraordinary things. How many of us know how to use this power? More importantly, how many of us know that this power exists?

First, we need to understand how the mind works and its power over us. Every time you try to step out of your comfort zone, your mind will generate all kinds of negative thoughts to keep you safe. Uncertainty and insecurity have no place in the mind of someone who knows their true nature. However, the mind acts as a self-defense mechanism every time you try something new.

Over time, we have been presented with different concepts regarding our mental activity and how this whole mental process influences our lives. So, I would like to present to you the version that is closest to my truth and the way I perceive it. Our mind is divided into three parts: conscious, subconscious, and superconscious. The first is the one that represents the aspect of the human mind that houses the immediate awareness a person possesses, which questions everything and which accepts or rejects ideas. The second is the part that accepts everything exactly as it perceives it and which influences the way we think, feel, and act. It also has a side known as the unconscious, which is hardly accessible to us, but which is in line with our beliefs and which has a significant impact on the way we operate.

While the conscious mind is the one we deliberately use in our daily activities and has the ability to generate and allow certain thoughts to dissolve or grow, the subconscious runs on autopilot, conditioned by our belief system, accepting and internalizing repetitive or emotionally impactful messages. The subconscious also activates itself through emotional memory, collects all the information it receives without judgment, and manages most of the things we do unconsciously. The first is based on reasoning and logic, while the second is rooted in memorized behaviors and habits, shaped by repressed beliefs and emotions, often without our conscious awareness. The superconscious refers to a higher state of consciousness that transcends both the conscious and subconscious mind, existing above the realm of ordinary human awareness. It is associated with spiritual insights, inspiration, and intuition. Through self-awareness, introspection, and the practice of mindfulness, we have the ability to enhance our consciousness and unlock higher states of understanding.

Scientists claim that the human mind is composed of two to four percent conscious and ninety-six to ninety-eight percent subconscious. The conscious mind is a small part of the human mind, but the way we can reprogram our subconscious is through our conscious mind, by bringing unconscious elements into awareness. The mind controls all aspects of our lives, which is why it is so important to understand how it works.

We have the ability to control the processes that occur in our thinking and choose to cultivate thoughts that are positive and constructive in nature, but most of us get stuck at this exact point because we don't see how we can do that. The solutions to all problems dwell in the depths of the subconscious, and each of us has exclusive access to infinite wisdom through our consciousness. We are responsible for all the emotional states we go through, by the nature of the thoughts we store in our subconscious. We create our entire inner universe, which flows outward through the power of our thoughts. Once you begin to understand this mechanism, you will experience absolute freedom, as you will no longer allow yourself to be controlled by the conditioning of the mental programming. Do not let yourself be influenced or overwhelmed by what comes from your programming and allow yourself to think big.

What we need to understand is that the struggle is not between the physical and mental elements of being, but rather between the mental and spiritual aspects of being. This fact implies an imbalance between them and can greatly influence the quality of our lives. As the ego rules our daily lives, and the spirit seeks a deeper purpose and connection, they are always in conflict. The importance of aligning and balancing these two aspects is crucial in order to live a more peaceful and fulfilling life.

The ego controls what we project into the outside world and is responsible for shaping a person's identity. It is largely made up of habits, beliefs, and subconscious principles. In simple terms, the ego is a collection of deep-seated assumptions and beliefs, and it also directs much of our programming. It holds a perspective on the world and forms opinions about life, but it does not necessarily experience it. It also has an influence on our thoughts and feelings, which deeply influences how we operate and the decisions we make. By being aware, acting accordingly, and overcoming the limitations of the ego, you can change and become that person worthy of admiration, like the one you hold in your visions.

If you try to figure it out through your conscious mind, you will never find the answer until you become truly aware. Awareness is the path to the supreme source of manifestation, and the only way to reach it is by following your heart. And how else, if not through love? God is love. As you open your heart to unconditional love, you will realize that it has always been within you, waiting to be remembered.

Does your mind or heart dictate your choices? Proverbs 23:7 translates roughly as follows: "For as he thinketh in his heart, so is he." Everything that happens in your subconscious defines you. Deep in your subconscious are your beliefs and values, as well as your fears and expectations. Any blessing or misfortune you experience is the result of your own mental harmony or disharmony. A man is what he believes and fears in the depths of his heart. Along this line, I would like to recall one of the most appreciated inspirational books of all time and which I recommend wholeheartedly. It is by the writer James Allen and the title, *As a Man Thinketh*, was inspired by the aforementioned verse. It highlights the power of thought and its impact on our character, circumstances, and overall success, including the cultivation of inner peace, serenity, and calmness.

You must be perfectly aligned with your higher self on every level. No matter what you do, how you feel, or what you think, you must live in harmony with your highest truth. Our thoughts hold immense creative power, but this power remains hidden when the intellect alone governs the body. Only when you rise above conditioning and transcend the physical and material realms will you return to your natural state and realize you are a limitless being with the ability to create the reality you desire.

Light Beings

You have to act beyond your rational thinking. The ego is the one that is always worried and that tends to get attached to things and people, that is always dissatisfied and constantly looking for excuses, and not you. By thinking this way, we are only operating from the lowest levels of consciousness. The best way is to diminish its power to interfere in the choices you make. I would say the ego is much like a child on the way to a campsite, constantly asking their parents: "Where are we now? Have we arrived, or are we at least close? How much longer until we get there?", impatient, curious, and full of questions about everything and everyone. Always be kind, tolerant, and warm-hearted toward it, but don't let it distract you from the path you're on.

You can become a better person and change these negative patterns that are dominating your behavior by learning to manage your thoughts and emotions. Otherwise, you will always be controlled by your programming, no matter how hard you try to resist it. It is like trying to swim against the current instead of flowing with it. When you operate under the guidance of your higher self, all programs cease, everything becomes still, and only silence and pure consciousness remain.

Imagine you are having dinner at a restaurant, and a beautiful song is playing in the background. But there is so much chatter at the surrounding tables that you cannot really hear it or enjoy it. Now, if you choose to stay quiet, focus your attention on the music, and tune out the noise, you will begin to hear it clearly. The same thing happens when your mind is overwhelmed with thoughts. By simply shifting your focus to what truly matters, you will be able to quiet the noise of the mind.

You need to start feeling worthy of well-being and prosperity, and believe that you deserve to attract good things into your life. But you won't truly feel this unless you're willing to grow and strive to become a better version of yourself. And how can you begin, if not by first discovering who you truly are? Once you truly know who you are, you rise above all limitations, and attachments no longer influence your future decisions.

The inner struggles you experience and the problems you believe you're facing belong to the ego, not to your true self. You come to realize that what you believed about yourself was never your true identity, but rather a collection of attachments, assumptions, and limiting beliefs. The first step is to consciously work on transforming yourself, aligning with the natural flow of the Universe. As you begin to access your creative power, everything changes. Only then will you be able to attract what you desire into your life effortlessly and with ease.

When you make a decision, pay attention to what your gut tells you to do and do it without thinking too much. You should always do it this way because the first thing that comes to your mind comes from the unknown, which is your intuitive mind. What follows comes from your rational mind and is based on the things you know and your past experiences. Our first instinct and inner voice are divine guidance, answers from beyond, and they deserve our attention, even when they surpass our worldly understanding. Trust your intuition without hesitation and follow it, because in that very moment, you are in direct communication with your higher self.

One day, I heard that a co-worker had bought a plot of land to build a house on. He spoke with such enthusiasm that it lit a flame of desire in both my heart and my partner's, and we began to dream of the same goal. I tracked month after month as the prices continued to rise and the more I postponed, the more impossible it seemed to me to achieve. A year passed, almost two, and I wondered if I didn't see a possibility before, how could I do it now when prices had almost doubled? Somehow deep down I knew it was possible and I refused to accept the idea that it wasn't. I told myself: "I don't know how, but I know that one way or another we will succeed. This is what I want and I will do whatever it takes." I held onto that vision with patience and trust, believing in its possibility. And one day, the opportunity presented itself and my partner and I managed to fulfill our dream. That was just the beginning. The most wonderful things came right after that, once we allowed ourselves to dream and chose to welcome the things we truly desired into our lives.

Something as simple as a house. Why do so many of us deny ourselves this joy? It is not an extraordinary dream, and yet for countless people, it remains just that. A dream. It is not life that holds us back, but our own unwillingness to believe we deserve more. And so, we settle for less than what we truly desire. Give love to what you long for, and you'll become a magnet for it.

What yesterday I thought was impossible to achieve, today seems to be a normality. We limit our potential because we make our plans in terms of what we think we are capable of doing rather than what we want. We are all capable of extraordinary things. Heart-driven decisions are more influential than mind-driven ones. We just have to figure out what it is that we truly want. No dream is too big to be fulfilled, so don't limit yourself to mediocre living just because you don't see how you could make it possible. Aim higher and keep on rising with every step and every thought.

Renew your mind by nourishing it with soul-enriching ideas. Reset your mindset and heart for the best. Set your intention to constantly raise your standards. That's the only way you can evolve. Once you grow as a person and become more deserving, your standards will also rise. Being aware of your worth and treating yourself accordingly is essential. The key is to maintain balance, as we often give so much to others that we end up neglecting ourselves or, at times, the opposite. You deserve to enjoy everything that makes your heart leap with joy, so allow yourself that freedom and trust that it is possible. There is nothing wrong with wanting more or longing for a more abundant life. It only becomes misaligned if the actions you take to get there are not rooted in that same goodness. God wants you to live well and to truly enjoy your journey in this world.

Seek solutions and inner guidance, and never lose your faith. Don't push away your desires, thinking they are too beautiful or too difficult to fulfill. Prepare yourself to receive everything in abundance and don't limit how much you believe is possible to receive. Patience is golden, and when it is paired with faith, miracles happen. This is how you bring your desires to life. By making it a habit to embrace wonderful truths, your entire life will begin to change tremendously. Along my path, I've come across a few quiet truths, and I would love to share them with you in this confession, through the paragraphs that follow.

All the aspirations and "I wants" you have can be seen as a form of self-analysis, but they are not necessarily the desire itself. The things you think will make you happy when they come true, in reality, may not. Desires are often based on the absence of those things, not on a true need. Ask yourself, is this what you really want, or is it something you feel you lack? First, reflect on why you crave it, whether it is a deep, burning desire that springs from within or just a fleeting craving you wish to satisfy. Make sure that what you want does not arise from a place of necessity, but rather from the soul. The answer lies within your heart.

If you want something, it means you don't have it yet, and if you place your desire in the future, the moment when it can be obtained will also be in the future. You will never see it accomplished unless you begin to see it happening right now. If you want to do something, you have to start today. There is no past and no future, there is only here and now. Every day is today, and so was yesterday. When tomorrow arrives, it will actually be today. Time is a continuum that helps us track events, their duration, and the intervals between them in this world. We live in a continuous present, which is why when we place our desires in the future, we automatically distance ourselves from them. By assuming that their fulfillment has not yet happened, we keep them in the near future indefinitely, and we may never experience them.

Much of the content of this book talks about the law of assumption, a concept brought to the public's attention by Neville Goddard. It is based on the idea that the reality in which we live is significantly influenced by assumptions, beliefs, and imagination. You can't achieve something if you don't think you're capable of doing it in the first place, and that's why most people give up before they even start. As a person's presumptions shift from uncertainty to confidence, success is inevitable. Whatever you assume to be your truth will manifest. Why? Because if you believe it can be achieved, then you will automatically start taking action on it. No one will do anything unless they first believe it can be done. When you truly decide to do something, everything in your environment aligns itself to support your desire and bring it to fruition.

Vivid visualization is the key to transcending boundaries and fulfilling our deepest desires. This means engaging all of the senses in the visualization process with the intention of creating a scene so vivid and detailed that it becomes a real lived experience. I guarantee it will work, and if it doesn't, the only reason is that it's not your truth. Let's say you set a new goal and you finally

The CREATOR

get very close to accomplishing it. The moment you start to feel like it's a typical state for you and see it as normal, only then will it happen and you will finally see that thing materialized.

Create a crystal-clear image of that thing you want from the bottom of your heart and focus on your desire. The power of thought will shape it. By spending time working in your mind with what you already know, you become more aware of how to create new ideas and then put them into action. An idea is given to you by the divine source and you have to put it on paper, otherwise it will disappear as soon as it arrives. You will not believe how many wonderful things come to your mind and have the power to change your conditioning, if only you become aware of them. You feel the need to constantly distract yourself because otherwise you think you will get bored, but you have to let your brain breathe and let the power of imagination come into play in order to create something. We are nothing without imagination. Everything in this world begins with the power of imagination. In the book *The Awakened Imagination*, Neville Goddard wrote: "Imagination is the very gateway to reality." All the things you desire reside within your imagination, and that is the very gateway to Heaven.

Do you let yourself be led by fear or faith? The power lies in the words, convictions, and expectations you have, and the result is achieved either through fear or faith. The fear we feel is not because things don't turn out the way we want. Things do not unfold the way we want because we're afraid. That's why things often don't come true; it's the fear we hold, not anything else.

When I started writing, I was afraid of how others would react, but I realized the desire was standing right behind that fear. At that time, I didn't think I could do it, but I made the decision to do it anyway. I was willing to give it a try, even though I had no idea how to do it, especially since I had never even written an article, so how could I possibly write a book? You won't get anywhere unless you cross the threshold of your fears. Also, don't wait for your work to be perfect, share it now. Perfection is an illusion, and if you keep waiting, you will miss the growth and the joy that come from the journey itself. Let your desires express themselves. Be stronger than the worries and limitations of the ego, and do what you truly want, as long as you uphold moral principles.

I occasionally get asked: "Luck seems to follow you, and everything flows so smoothly for you. What's your secret?" I tell them that I think everything comes down to faith, but most interrupt and say: "No, seriously, how do you do this?"

It's not about being lucky, it's all about faith and conviction, but we tend to confuse hope with faith. There was a time when I believed that hope and faith were interchangeable, but I've come to realize they are not the same. While both are deeply connected, they are distinct in their essence. Faith is the power and conviction that you invest in the unknown, and hope could be called the result of the desire for a future situation. Faith means believing in the existence of something you cannot even see. Hope means trusting that what you believe in will eventually come to fruition. You cannot have hope without faith, just as faith alone, without the active anticipation of the future, remains incomplete. Faith provides the foundation, and hope fuels the journey toward realizing what you believe is possible.

Notice the difference between "I hope everything will turn out well" and "I believe everything will turn out well". The first, although operating on the basis of a strong optimistic impulse and expecting a positive outcome, always seems to have a slightly negative connotation and where a trace of pessimism can be felt, and the latter is of a positive nature and in which the person seems confident that everything will turn out well in the end. However, believing and having the certainty that it will eventually come true is, in the end, the key to manifesting what you want.

Knowledge is immeasurable and infinitely more powerful than anything else. The main distinction between knowing and believing lies the degree of trust attributed to each. When you say: "I believe that..." it hides a slight doubt and seems to be more of an opinion, but not something you're necessarily convinced of. On the other hand, when you say: "I know that..." it is something certain and of which you are absolutely sure. When you say: "I know (something)" it's not merely something you've learned. Instead, it's a glimmer of consciousness, a deep inner knowing that comes with the certainty that it will be so. This knowing transcends intellectual understanding and connects with a profound truth that assures its manifestation. When we move beyond hope and faith into knowing, we no longer seek but become.

According to Neale Donald Walsch, there are three levels of awareness: hope, faith, and knowledge. A simple way to illustrate this could be: "I hope I can do it", "I believe I can do it", and "I know I can do it". Can you see the difference? These levels reflect the way we grow in our understanding and confidence. For example, when approaching a goal, we might first say, "I hope I can do it." As we gain more confidence, "I know I can do it." This progression represents the journey from uncertainty to certainty; from hope to knowledge.

Knowledge is not merely the accumulation of facts, but the silent illumination of pure consciousness, surpassing all forms.

It is the summit where understanding dissolves into being. Yet, just as hope forms the foundation of faith, faith itself is the essential basis of knowledge. When you operate from this level of awareness, your experience is no longer dependent on external circumstances or outcomes. Instead, you live from a profound inner knowing, deeply connected to the divine essence within you. This alignment brings a sense of certainty and peace, beyond what the world around you can offer.

And now, returning to the imagination, what we see around us is the direct projection of our mind. As I mentioned in the previous chapters, our own reality is shaped by the mental images that our thoughts produce. The words you use will dictate your end. We must use words wisely, for they have the power to shape our reality.

Whenever I felt tired, I would often tell myself: "I am tired" and the more I repeated it, the more the feeling would grow, as if I were reinforcing my exhaustion. Yet, everything shifted once I realized that I am not my body. The moment you understand this truth, a powerful transformation occurs. You begin to recognize that it is the body that is tired, not you. Then, you will start telling yourself: "I am full of energy, but my body needs to recharge." By separating your sense of identity from the physical body and accepting that it simply needs rest, you can tap into an inner wellspring of energy. It's a remarkable shift. Once you change your perspective and recognize that you are not bound by the limitations of your body, your approach to life changes entirely.

Developing the right mindset and attitude toward oneself will result in a positive attitude toward life. "I am" are the words that describe our beliefs. The sentences that begin with these two words, and their completion, create the reality in which one lives. The essence of our being is created by the "I am", which establishes all that we truly are and which also exposes what our soul is made of.

The secret lies in the love you radiate into the world. Love expresses itself through gratitude, and when we fill our hearts with love, we find ourselves centered. Your body, mind, soul, and spirit will all align in harmony as you follow your heart. Gratitude will lift up your soul. You just need to reach this point. Gratitude is the key that connects your soul to the source of infinite abundance, elevating you to the highest vibrational energy. Happiness resides in this connection, and as long as you follow it, you will succeed, but it's always grounded in your own sense of worthiness.

Many manifestation practitioners believe that the best times for meditation are just before bed or right after waking up, because our mind is more open and less obstructed by unconscious barriers. The moment right before falling asleep is the perfect time to plant your idea and imagine yourself actually living and experiencing the life of your dreams. In the fifth chapter, I mentioned how important it is to practice gratitude and I have to say that the best way to do it is during the first hour in the morning, right after you wake up, because it is when you are deciding how you will spend your day and this way you go into the day with good intentions and positive energy. If possible, you can also dedicate some time during the day as that will generate even more impact in your life.

I discovered that right before bed is the ideal time to reflect. The final hour before I intend to go to bed is when I go over my day and reflect back on my thoughts. The most crucial moment of the day is the five minutes just before you fall asleep. A while ago, I created a bedtime routine focused on vitality and regeneration, a practice I still use today to restore my body. How does this work? I go to sleep with the belief that my body will heal itself while I rest. This idea came to me years ago when I first encountered Joseph Murphy's teachings about the power of the subconscious mind and the many miraculous healing cases he discussed. Dr. Joe Dispenza perfectly sums this up with the statement, "The power that made the body, heals the body." You may have heard his remarkable story, in which he healed himself using the power of his mind and the practice of visualizing a full recovery. This story serves as a powerful reminder of how powerful we truly are and how crucial it is to understand how to channel this energy for our benefit. In truth, nothing has the power to heal or harm us more than our imagination.

Close your eyes and focus on your body before bed to enter a meditative state. Release any attachments and begin to imagine the things you wish to manifest in your life. I often seek guidance and clarity in my visions during the precise moment when we transition from the waking state to the dream state. This unique stage of consciousness allows reprogramming to occur on a much deeper level, as the barriers between imagination and reality dissolve, heightening the power of manifestation. Neville Goddard, one of the most influential teachers in history, taught that imagination is the key to manifestation and by using it effectively, we can use it to create anything we desire in our lives. He recommended the technique of vivid visualization, which involves experiencing the future in the present, in order to manifest one's deepest desires.

Prayer is not about sitting on your knees and asking God to help you. Prayer is done through imagination and what we ask for is what we think about all the time. Through imagination we communicate with God. No matter what is behind the images that arise in our minds, whether they are based on faith or fear, we ask for them when we visualize them. This is actually what we call prayer, and it is the only way to tell God what we want to receive and manifest. Even if it's not what we truly want, by using this power, we create it. Every action we take, every thought we have, involves imagination. Try to think about something without using your imagination and you will see that it is impossible for you to do it. When you think, you don't do it through words, but through images in action. If you don't like what you attract into your life, then you need to change your thoughts and the images you keep alive in your mind. That's why it's so important to understand this and it is that simple. The question is, do you believe this is possible? There is only one way to find out.

I've been dreaming of a figure of light who told me that abundance flows infinitely right in front of me and so if I want to enjoy it, the only thing I have to do is to step forward. To be part of greatness. I've been working on my book cover concept for months, changing it over and over until one day it just came out of nowhere. That night, I set it on my smartphone's lock screen and went to sleep. I was wondering, what's the meaning? I had a revolutionary experience while sleeping that night, but one thing worth mentioning, as weird as it sounds, is what this voice was saying out loud: "You are now connected with Bob," and when I woke up, I looked at my screen to see the time and I saw the image, clearer than ever. What I've created represents a reinterpretation of the image of the mind and body, a symbol that was introduced to Bob Proctor decades ago by one of his mentors and you can find this concept everywhere in his material, especially when he talks about two of my favorite topics: paradigm and attitude. If you're looking for a starting point, his work is definitely worth exploring to understand how the mind works.

Light Beings

I believe that somehow, we are all linked by the same divine essence, sharing a deeper bond that transcends the physical realm. We receive answers to our questions all the time, but are we truly listening?

If you would just look up, you could see it. But we often think that God resides somewhere in the sky, separate from us. In reality, He lives through us, lodged in our hearts. Our only mission in this world is to recognize Him and realize that He made us co-creators. How do you want to live from now on? Simply do what resonates with your soul, let the power flow, and allow its beauty to expand. In doing so, your life will unfold in ways even better than you ever imagined. Remember, everything will unfold as you have believed.

Whenever I encounter a blockage, I visualize myself standing in front of a door. On the other side of this door lies abundance overflowing with light, joy, and opportunity, all waiting for me. But the door won't open fully. I notice something is wedged at the bottom, keeping it stuck. As soon as I become aware of it, I gently remove the obstruction. Instantly, the door swings wide open, and a flood of light and abundance pours over me, embracing me fully. I return to this practice whenever I feel stuck, gently reminding myself to let go, clear the way, and allow all the good life has to offer to flow freely into my experience.

Be light. This is the most wonderful message I have for you, my dear friend. I love the depth of this sentence, for it holds a multitude of meanings. Be light in your mind, body, soul, and spirit. Knowing that you have the ability to choose to let go of feelings that don't serve you allows you to become lighter and make space within to be filled with love, peace, and light.

Now, there is one question left to be answered: What makes an individual's experience of life so different from another's? There is so much to be discovered, yet I've come to realize that the quality of human life stands in one word: connection. The great law of life is love, and through love comes all blessings. Let every action you take come from the heart. The key ingredient in any recipe is love. Are you immersed in light or darkness? Be light in all ways.

May God bless every step you take on your luminous path, and may all your heart's desires be fulfilled. May you be blessed with abundance in all its forms, and may your journey be filled with joy, light, and love. Until next time, with gratitude, your companion.

Keep on rising and doing things that light up your soul.

You are a radiant light being.

References

Throughout this book, I've drawn on powerful words, timeless wisdom, and thought-provoking ideas from a variety of sources. I remain deeply grateful to these voices, quotes and concepts that have supported and inspired the messages shared here.

Allen, James. *As a Man Thinketh*. 1st ed. London: The Castle Press, 1902.

Aurelius, Marcus. *Meditations*. Translated by George Long. London: George Bell and Sons, 1862.

Blake, William. *Jerusalem: The Emanation of the Giant Albion*. 1820.

Byrne, Rhonda. *The Secret*. 1st ed. New York: Atria, 2006.

Canfield, Jack. "The Power of Being Committed." Jack Canfield, 2021. https://jackcanfield.com/blog/being-committed/.

Dispenza, Joe. "Becoming Divine." Dr Joe Dispenza, 2019. https://drjoedispenza.com/dr-joes-blog/becoming-divine

Emerson, Ralph Waldo. *Compensation*. In *Essays: First Series*, 1841. Public domain edition via Project Gutenberg. https://www.gutenberg.org/ebooks/2944

Gallagher, Sandy. "Seven Universal Laws at a Glance." Proctor Gallagher Institute, 2024. https://proctorgallagherinstitute.com/universal-laws/seven-universal-laws-at-a-glance/.

Goddard, Neville. *Awakened Imagination*. 1954.

Goddard, Neville. *The Power of Awareness*. 1952.

Hill, Napoleon. *Think and Grow Rich: The Original, an Official Publication of the Napoleon Hill Foundation*. Sound Wisdom, 2016.

Pico Della Mirandola, Giovanni. *Oration on the Dignity of Man*. Regnery Publishing, 1956.

Murphy, Joseph. *The Power of Your Subconscious Mind*. Englewood Cliffs, NJ: Prentice-Hall, 1963.

Nightingale, Earl. *The Strangest Secret*. Audio version, Nightingale-Conant, 1956.

Piers Morgan Uncensored. "The FULL Cristiano Ronaldo Interview with Piers Morgan | Parts 1 and 2." YouTube, November 18, 2022. https://www.youtube.com/watch?v=Jk9uJRMvBIA&ab_channel=PiersMorganUncensored.

Proctor, Bob. "Are You Tired of Feeling Stuck?" Proctor Gallagher Institute, 1 Nov. 2024, https://proctorgallagherinstitute.com/unstuck/are-you-tired-of-feeling-stuck/.

Proctor Gallagher Institute. "Law of Vibration (Full Lesson) | Bob Proctor." YouTube, April 12, 2021. https://www.youtube.com/watch?v=-ENj3vyFvKo.

Proctor, Bob. "Snap Decisions and Small Things." Proctor Gallagher Institute, 2024. https://proctorgallagherinstitute.com/decision/snap-decisions-and-small-things.

Proctor, Bob. "The Real Secret to Living the Life You Want." Proctor Gallagher Institute, 8 Dec. 2024, https://proctorgallagherinstitute.com/the-secret/the-real-secret-to-living-the-life-you-want/.

Rolland, Romain. *Beethoven: The Creator*. Translated by Ernest Hull, Henry Holt and Company, 1929.

The Holy Bible: King James Version. Thomas Nelson, 1987.

The Secret by Rhonda Byrne. "Everything Is Possible | RHONDA LIVE 4." YouTube, July 6, 2021. https://www.youtube.com/watch?v=5J8eCR60KxE.

Walsch, Neale Donald. *Conversations with God: An Uncommon Dialogue*, Books 1–3. New York: G.P. Putnam's Sons, 1995–1998.

Wattles, Wallace D. *The Science of Getting Rich*. Elizabeth Towne Company, 1910.

Recommended Reading

If you're looking to continue your personal growth journey, these books are a great place to start, along with the ones cited in the references section. Each one has offered me insight, encouragement, or practical tools, and I hope they serve you as meaningfully as they have served me.

Assaraf, John. *Having It All: Achieving Your Life's Goals and Dreams*. Atria Books, 2007.

Byrne, Rhonda. *The Greatest Secret*. HarperCollins, 2020.

Byrne, Rhonda. *The Power*. Simon & Schuster, 2010.

Canfield, Jack, and Janet Switzer. *The Success Principles: How to Get from Where You Are to Where You Want to Be*. 10th ed. New York: William Morrow and Company, 2015.

de Mello, Anthony. *Awareness*. Fount, 1997.

Dispenza, Joe. *Becoming Supernatural*. Hay House, 2019.

Dispenza, Joe. *Breaking the Habit of Being Yourself: How to Lose Your Mind and Create a New One*. Hay House, 2012.

Dispenza, Joe. *You Are the Placebo: Making Your Mind Matter*. Hay House, 2014.

Dyer, Wayne W. *Change Your Thoughts, Change Your Life: Living the Wisdom of the Tao*. Hay House, 2007.

Goddard, Neville. *The Neville Collection: All 10 Books by a Modern Master*. Grapevine, 2022.

Maharshi, Ramana. *The Collected Works of Ramana Maharshi*. Translated by Arthur Osborne. 10th ed. Sophia Perennis et Universalis, 2006.

Maltz, Maxwell. *Psycho-Cybernetics Deluxe Edition: The Original Text of the Classic Guide to a New Life*. J.P. Tarcher, U.S./Perigee Bks, 2016.

Méndez, Conny. *The Little Blue Book Aka El Librito Azul: Metaphysics in Simple Terms*. Translated by Alio Publishing Group. Alio Publishing Group, 2023.

Nightingale, Earl. *Lead the Field*. Sound Wisdom, 2018.

Pritchett, Price. *You^2: A High-Velocity Formula for Multiplying Your Personal Effectiveness in Quantum Leaps*. Pritchett & Associates, 1994.

Proctor, Bob. *Change Your Paradigm, Change Your Life*. G&D Media, 2021.

Proctor, Bob. *You Were Born Rich*. Life Success Pacific Rim, 2003.

Proctor, Brian. *My Father Knew the Secret: Growing up with Bob Proctor*. KellyProctorCo, 2023.

Proctor, Bob, and Sandy Gallagher. *The Secret of the Science of Getting Rich: Change Your Beliefs about Success and Money to Create the Life You Want*. G&D Media, 2022.

Tracy, Brian. *Believe It to Achieve It: Overcome Your Doubts, Let Go of the Past, and Unlock Your Full Potential*. Tarcherperigee, 2017.

About the Author

Born in 1993 in Romania, Cosmina Movilescu has been living in the UK since late 2018 alongside her fiancé and an ever-growing collection of books. Her fascination with the human mind began after watching *The Secret* documentary by Rhonda Byrne, and she's been on a mission to figure out life ever since. This curiosity led her to explore the wisdom of great thinkers and the profound impact of the mind on our daily lives. Passionate about personal growth, she continues to research and discover ways to create a more fulfilling existence. A warm and curious soul, she loves books, good food, and meaningful connections. Through her writing, Cosmina strives to inspire others to embrace a lighter, more effortless way of living. If her words resonate with you, she would love to hear from you. Please feel free to reach out, share your thoughts, or simply say hello.

Instagram: @belight.soul | Cosmina Movilescu

Email: worldwide.belight@gmail.com

www.ingramcontent.com/pod-product-compliance
Lightning Source LLC
Chambersburg PA
CBHW060400080526
44583CB00012B/403